RECREATING MARRIAGE
WITH THE SAME OLD SPOUSE

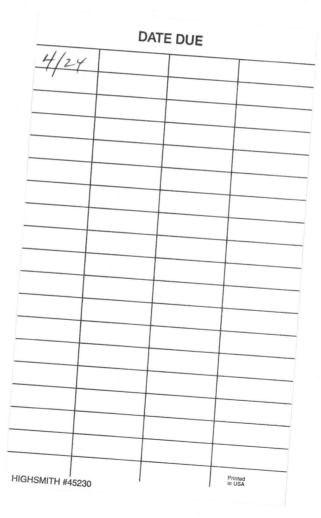

DATE DUE

4/24			

HIGHSMITH #45230   Printed in USA

RECREATING MARRIAGE
WITH THE
SAME OLD SPOUSE

A GUIDE FOR COUPLES

SANDRA GRAY BENDER, PH.D.

Westminster John Knox Press
Louisville, Kentucky

Scripture quotations from the New Revised Standard Version
of the Bible are copyright © 1989 by the Division of Christian Education
of the National Council of the Churches of Christ in the U.S.A.
and are used by permission.

Book design by Jennifer K. Cox
Cover design by Kevin Darst
Cover illustration: Middle-aged couple.
G. Fritz. Courtesy of SuperStock.

First edition
Published by Westminster John Knox Press
Louisville, Kentucky

This book is printed on acid-free paper that meets the
American National Standards Institute Z39.48 standard. ∞

PRINTED IN THE UNITED STATES OF AMERICA
97 98 99 00 01 02 03 04 05 06 — 10 9 8 7 6 5 4 3 2 1

Library of Congress Cataloging-in-Publication Data

Bender, Sandra Gray, date.
     Recreating marriage with the same old spouse : a guide for couples
/ Sandra Gray Bender — 1st ed.
          p.   cm.
     Includes bibliographical references.
     ISBN 0-664-25726-7 (alk. paper)
     1. Marriage.   2. Communication in marriage.   3. Married people—
Psychology.   4. Marriage—Religious aspects.   I. Title.
HQ734.B53   1997
646.7′8—dc21   96-52259

Contents

Preface

When I was a little girl, I wanted to be a housewife just like my mother. (This was before she worked outside our home.) I played with dolls, toy sets of china, and other miniature household items. However, life circumstances and my own personality converged to create the fear that as a grown-up I would never have the family that I wanted. Moving around a lot as a Navy kid increased my natural shyness. I did not make friends easily. When we finally settled into a rural community in Mississippi, I felt very different from the other kids. I was definitely not the kind of girl who was going to be popular with boys. I was too independent, too big, too smart, and not athletic.

By age 14, I felt I had little hope of fulfilling my dream of becoming a housewife, so I did what I was good at—studying. An interest in science led me to nursing school, which dealt another blow to my dream of having a family of my own. The only men on campus were medical students. They were four years older and a lot more experienced in life. But that was not the only problem. I held strong opinions and did not know how to communicate them gracefully to men who had their own strong opinions and expected women to fall in line. I looked forward to attending graduate school to study psychology, where I hoped to find more communicative and accepting men.

Psychology was appealing, probably because I felt I had special talents with people and an intense need to learn about people. I had some deficits though. I felt unlovable. I did not know how to express authentically what I was really feeling, and I possessed all the usual cultural problems, including an unworkable set of beliefs about relationships and an inability to negotiate differences. A friend once said, "Psychologists take their weakness and turn it into a career." Perhaps she is right. All psychologists do grow up with the same deficits shared by everyone in the culture. However, we psychologists have a peculiar need to understand how people work.

I immersed myself in relationship training through the Gestalt Institute of Cleveland, which I entered simultaneously with graduate school. I received my Ph.D. from Case Western Reserve University in 1971. The same year I married my first husband and acquired a stepson, Dylan, who lived with us. Three years later I gave birth to a daughter, Ariana. When I married, I thought I had all the answers about marriage. That belief—and my marriage—came to a humiliating end after a mere five years. I was back in the fix of not knowing how to conduct a marriage that worked and yet wanting a family very much.

Instead of having answers, I had questions. I lived through several relationships with men, hoping each was "the one." I learned from every relationship and every failure. I examined each relationship as though observing a jewel with many facets. I asked each partner what went wrong and each responded generously. I went to popular human relations training seminars, such as National Training Labs, Weir Labs, est, and the Forum. Among the professional leaders with whom I trained were Gestalt therapists (Fritz and Laura Perls, Erving and Miriam Polster, and Joseph Zinker), marriage and family therapists (Carl Whitaker, Virginia Satir, Jay Haley, William Masters, and Virginia Johnson), and Neurolinguistic Programmers (Richard Grinder, John Bandler, Leslie Cameron Bandler, and Robert Dilts).

As I was making a psychological exploration of relationships, I also explored the spiritual realm. My spiritual parents were Henry Andersen, senior pastor, and Carolyn Mikels, associate pastor of Fairmount Presbyterian Church in Cleveland Heights, Ohio. Hank and Carolyn demonstrated God's love to me constantly and had faith in my spiritual journey.

I approached my thirty-ninth birthday with grief for the marriage I thought I would never have. After a year of sadness, I turned forty uneventfully, ready to accept the rest of my life. I was grateful for the friends who were intimate enough to celebrate holidays and go on vacations with me and support me in rearing my daughter and stepson. My friends had become my family.

After several friends told me of professional women who had advertised in the "Personal" section of *Cleveland Magazine* and had married men whom they had met, I decided I had nothing to lose by trying it. I placed my ad and met several nice men, including my present husband, Nate, and the rest is history.

Nate has a Ph.D. in psychology and is a Licensed Professional Clinical Counselor. In spite of our advanced degrees, we both had a lot to learn about creating a relationship. Nate was willing to learn about relationships by creating one with me. We went to seminars to learn relationship skills. We began a group for divorced persons, Starting Anew, at

Fairmount Presbyterian Church, and taught and shared what we were learning while developing ourselves. We struggled with the complicated issues involved in having blended families. And we had the usual problems that result when two different kinds of people try to live together.

Both of us were self-sufficient people and prided ourselves on being able to survive alone. Each of us had to give up some of our personal style in order to put our family together. We felt severely intruded upon in our efforts to make way for each other.

I had been divorced for nine years and Nate for four years when we met. Nate and I already had our individual styles. Some things about him worked well for me. He is friendly, tolerant, patient, and has a high level of commitment. But other things didn't work for me. While I appreciated his loving attitude toward his ten-year-old son, Jon, it led him to be very tolerant of what I considered unmannerly and insubordinate behavior. Nate also seemed blind to clutter, while I liked a very organized household. And, of course, he found me wanting on occasion: Nate is an athlete and believes in pushing himself and others to increase endurance. He believes in getting up at the crack of dawn to exercise and get to work. He thought my permitting Ariana (my twelve-year-old daughter) and Dylan (my twenty-one-year-old stepson from my previous marriage) to "sleep in" was evidence of my overindulgence. I reacted to Nate's expanding his work hours as an effort to install me as housekeeper and baby-sitter and then abandon me. Fur flew. *This* was the family I wanted so badly?

We continued to communicate. Both of us were committed to being together for the rest of our lives—and to having a good time doing it. We knew there must be a way to work out these differences, even if we did not know how at the time. Our persistence paid off as we held family meetings and made new rules together. It took Ariana a year to lower her surly guard and trust that we were indeed a family. Jon, Nate's son, welcomed me from the beginning. He just refused to do anything I asked of him. This smoothed out a bit over time as I proved I was strong and his dad supported me, but I still wanted more compliance than what came naturally to this strong-willed boy.

Perfect we aren't, but family life has emerged from the stormy and exhausting days when we were working at it all the time to a genuine enjoyment of life together as the kids become competent and independent. During our eight years of marriage, Dylan has graduated from college and moved several times to seek his fortune. He has probably settled in Denver in the restaurant business. Ariana is a junior in college, presently in Indonesia and places beyond as she studies different cultures. Jon is just beginning to study fish and wildlife in college. When Jon leaves for college, Nate and I will be alone together for the first time in our married life. But the last eight years have been very precious. This family feels natural, like we really belong together. It is a haven from which children can launch.

Nate and I started sharing what we were learning about relationships with a class—Recreating Marriage—for marriage enrichment at our church, Fairmount Presbyterian Church. This book grew out of weekly plans for that class. We want others to benefit from our hard-won experience. We also want to prevent other couples from going through the pain of divorce, which has to be one of the most difficult experiences in life.

The foundation for this course was laid in my childhood by Hugh and Carolyn Gray, my parents, both endowed with great spiritual depth and unshakable faith. Being able to start my own spiritual journey from that platform has been priceless, and I am grateful. A special acknowledgment goes to Nate. His thoughts and behavior are portrayed throughout this book. I appreciate our children for participating in the adventure of life with us and living with some motherly neglect while I sat at my computer. The stories of Ariana, Dylan, and Jon are part of this book since they are an intimate part of our marriage. I also acknowledge those couples who have participated in Recreating Marriage. They have been the cocreators of this project. They have informed us about what was important for them to learn. They had faith in us when we were newly married and figuring out what to do. They told us what parts of the program worked and what did not work. I am grateful to Connie Schultz, whose superb interviewing and writing skills gave me confidence and made this project a joy. Finally, I appreciate Stephanie Egnotovich, my editor at Westminster John Knox Press, who recognized the value of the ideas, coached me on writing clearly, and helped transform *Recreating Marriage* into this book.

Introduction

This book is about love. Most people feel love of one kind or another for their spouse when they get married. As time goes on, that wonderful feeling can erode because a couple is not successful in creating a relationship they both enjoy. The remark I often hear from separating couples is "I don't love him (or her) anymore." I interpret that statement to mean "I did not know how to behave and communicate in such a way that we continued the loving feelings we had in the beginning." This course is an attempt to create skills two people can use to perpetually revitalize the loving bond between them. For some couples this course will enrich an already rewarding relationship. For other couples it may seem like waking the dead, the deadness they have felt between them for years.

Recreating Marriage is written for couples who want to enhance and develop their skills for marriage. It may be used as a course for couples who want to study with or without a group. A group situation is often helpful because interacting with other people enables couples to gain perspective by hearing other people share. Couples also have the opportunity to deepen friendships beyond the usual sharing of facts and opinions about matters external to themselves, such as sports and children's activities. A logical place for a group to be formed is within a church or synagogue. For some couples, private explorations together will be preferable. Some couples use the material as a way to have interesting conversations while on long car trips or weekend getaways.

I have called the course "Recreating Marriage" because every marriage is in a state of continuous change, as are the persons who create the marriage. Most people do not take control of that change but let it happen spontaneously and, at times, without control. As we can see by the divorce rate, spontaneous change is not necessarily change for the better. People can move in different directions and the resulting distance can feel like falling out of love. Married people need intentional direction for change so that partners are sure they are creating what they want. Marriages have the pressures of births, raising children, and living with them through all stages of their development; spouses' careers; parents' aging and dying; fluctuations in finances; and the aging of the spouses, all of which require change from the young couple full of love and hope at the time of their marriage. Couples who have a strong commitment to each other but fear they have "fallen out of love" can profit from *Recreating Marriage* by affirming the growth that has taken place while they have been emotionally distant and by learning skills to bridge the differences.

This book revolves around the concept of identity. Our identity continuously evolves as we experience life and develop perspective about ourselves, unless we hold on tight to rigid ideas about ourselves and determine never to change. Our identity determines our behavior. For example, when clients tell me they are suffering from low self-esteem, what they mean is they have negative beliefs about themselves. Those negative beliefs interfere with every aspect of their lives, including their close relationships.

Recreating Marriage is about focusing on ways to think about yourself positively, as a glorious reflection of God's creation. You begin by examining the roles you play, which represent your identity, and the Myers-Briggs Personality Types, which are categories of personality types based on the theories of Swiss psychologist Carl Jung. Confidence in developing a satisfying relationship is further enhanced by learning communication skills and exploring beliefs and values. You will begin to see emotions as the barometer of well-being rather than as the essence of your being. Skills for managing conflicts are practiced. Ultimately, you and your spouse will open the way for a life of love and emotional fulfillment.

My purpose is to help you explore and discuss your beliefs, not to tell you what to believe. I refer at times to religious beliefs. I have included them because religious beliefs are a primary motivator for most people, even if they are not aware of it. Even those people who have never participated in an organized religion grew up in a culture that contains religious beliefs. At the very least, we concluded either that there is some organization and unity to the process of life or that life is random and meaningless. It is our beliefs about the meaning of life and how we fit into that meaning that I refer to as "religion." My background is Southern Methodist, and I am currently Presbyterian. However, the process of exploring beliefs in relationship to eternal truths is one in which persons practicing any religion—or no religion—can participate.

Throughout the book I have used my family as examples in order to create credibility. We are a complicated family with three children from three different marriages. We have used these techniques, refining the process as we learned from our experience. We are not only experts with psychology degrees but are also people with the same difficulties that you face. Many people have told us, "If you can do it, so can I." I have also included many examples based on clients' marriages. The people and situations are composites; no one is named or exactly described, but the situations are accurate.

Discussions and *Exercises* appear throughout the book. The discussion questions lead you to explore your thoughts and feelings about issues being discussed, creating more intimacy in the process. You will never again have to look at your spouse over the dinner table and not have anything to say if you can recall a discussion or exercise, such as "I'd like you to affirm me for all the work I put into painting the bathroom," or "I'd like you to listen reflectively while I tell you about a problem I'm having with our son." (The technique we call "reflective listening" is explained in chapter 6.) The Exercises demonstrate communication processes and provide step-by-step instruction to enable you to develop your skills.

Recreating Marriage is education, not psychotherapy. (I use the terms *psychotherapy* and *counseling* interchangeably in this book.) This book is for couples who do not have serious emotional deficits, simply because people who are overwhelmed emotionally are not able to focus. Couples who are considering divorce or have an emotionally distraught spouse should seek professional counseling. If you are bothered by strong negative feelings about yourself or your spouse, ask someone you trust, such as your clergy person or physician, to recommend a therapist. You can find a list of qualified therapists in your telephone book under your local psychological association, or call the Association of Marriage and Family Therapists (202-452-0109) for a referral. Some people, such as abused children or adult children of alcoholics, may have negative identities. In most communities there are support groups and Twelve Step programs to help with these problems. These groups have no membership fees and can be contacted through Alcoholics Anonymous.

Inviting Your Spouse to Participate

Give a simple invitation to your partner. Review the outline of the program first, and inspire your partner with your hopes for an enriched relationship. Talk about some of the changes you want. Ask your partner what kind of changes he or she would wanted. Discuss how each of you would feel if you had the kind of marriage you want. Refrain from any suggestion of blame. Many spouses will be delighted and encouraged by your invitation.

The only real problem may be time. You will have to make time in your lives in a way that suits you and your partner, and you will have to plan specific times or you won't get around to it. You can take the book on car and plane trips to create conversations. You can set aside a regular time during the week. You can go to a quiet vacation place and go through the entire book.

Often, one spouse is more interested in education about the relationship than the other. This can easily be the case if one partner is having his or her needs met and the other partner is not. For the resistant partner, the idea of change may imply giving up something very important. Reassure your partner that Recreating Marriage teaches ways to work issues out so that both partners win. A common conflict, for example, occurs when one spouse values social activities only in couples and the other wants friendships outside the couple. Although the relationships would not be sexual, the change can be frightening to the person left at home. It may be hard to imagine that solutions can be found that will be reassuring to both partners, but they can.

You can involve your spouse in developing your marriage, even if she or he will not formally read and discuss this book or attend a group. First, if your spouse will not participate in structured Recreating Marriage discussions, bring up questions casually. Write your answers to Discussion questions in your journal and do Exercises in preparation for talking with your spouse. Tell him or her what you are learning. Conversations will immediately become more interesting. Who could resist, "I read about appreciation today. I want to tell you something that I appreciate about you." One person who learns relationship skills can have a powerful effect on the other.

Second, recognize that *change in your own behavior can change your spouse's behavior.* It is not unusual for one spouse to want to learn relationship skills but the other to be uninterested. One person can strongly influence a positive relationship if she or he is willing to accept that challenge. When you change, the relationship shifts in response. For example, if you and your partner argue a lot, and you start using reflective listening, the relationship has altered without your spouse "cooperating" an ounce. Imagine what would happen if you stopped complaining! Or if you expressed your feelings without implying that your spouse caused them.

Third, recognize that *time is a resource.* The way you communicate and live took years to develop. It will take some time to reorganize. If you are willing to change but your partner isn't, don't give up. If your partner has not been expressing love for some time, do not expect a positive response just because you begin to express appreciation and affirmations. It may be months before your partner can trust that your new behavior will last and be willing to open up. Believe that positive change is inevitable if you continue your own spiritual and personal growth path.

Fourth, *find other people* to support the positive communication skills you are learning. Share this book with friends and relatives. Talk with them about what you are learning. Practice communication skills with other people in your life besides your spouse.

Fifth, *recognize the power of the marital bond.* Many partners "throw in the towel" because they believe their partner does not care. I have developed a belief about the marital bond over years of being a marital therapist. The bond between two people who have opened themselves at one point in their lives enough to dream a common dream and commit their lives to each other is like a magnet, drawing them toward each other no matter what the circumstances. The vulnerability can also produce a resistance and defensiveness that no other relationship contains, but that is further evidence of this "magnetism" between marital partners. Many people give up on their marriages because they hurt so much. The pain, too, is a result of the bond.

Recreating Marriage will be a beginning. It will take a lot of time and effort. Be patient with yourself and with your spouse as you learn new methods of relating. Your present ways of talking with each other seem natural, even though they may be ineffective. It will take practice to be comfortable with new tools. Some couples have repeated the course Recreating Marriage for years to reinforce new habits. Should you change all your present ways of talking with each other? Of course not. Only when you run into trouble should you think about finding a new way of speaking or negotiating that is more effective.

Then, of course, you have to continue applying what you have learned for the rest of your lives. But what better reward for your effort than a life with vitality and a happy marriage?

How to Use This Book

Recreating Marriage will take you on a journey of marital and spiritual enrichment. You will have an opportunity for very personal encounters with each other, with yourself, and with God. The landscape on this journey will be your ideas, thoughts, and feelings, and your equipment will be this book, conversations with each other, and your journal. You will be exploring your own experience and sharing yourself with your partner.

Recreating Marriage is written so that it can be used by a couple or a group of couples. Studying with a group is an effective, interesting, and heartwarming method of learning about marriage. You will hear of a variety of ways of behaving in a marriage, which will broaden your perspective and provide you with humor and tolerance toward yourself. You will never have to share anything embarrassing or anything you want to keep private. You will discover what is special about your own marriage. Participating in a group enriches your life with open and genuine conversations with other couples.

If you are interested in belonging to a Recreating Marriage group, give a copy of this book to your pastor, priest, or rabbi. Suggest that he or she provide a Recreating Marriage group for your congregation. (For more information on Recreating Marriage retreat weekends, write to Recreating Marriage, P.O. Box 18433, Cleveland Heights, OH 44118-0433 or e-mail bender@en.com.)

Purchase a notebook for each of you to use as a journal. In your journal you will write answers to some questions and exercises before you share them with your partner. Some exercises build on former ones, so you will need to have all your answers available as you proceed.

Wives (although there are some exceptional husbands) will usually initiate this project and carry it through to completion. It is common for one person to initiate the conversations. This does not mean the other person has less love; he or she simply has different ways of showing it. If participating in Recreating Marriage is your idea, be willing to accept that it is your gift to the relationship, and do not expect your spouse to feel the same inspiration that you do.

When you initiate Recreating Marriage conversations, timing is critical. Be sure you have your partner's attention. If your partner has agreed to go through the book, you can ask directly for conversations about the Discussions and Exercises in sequence. Tell him or her you want to have a Recreating Marriage conversation and set a convenient time. If you find that you do not have time to talk, which happens in two-career families with children, make time to go out together at least once a week. You can have more productive conversations in your precious time by discussing the Recreating Marriage questions instead of complaining about the hassles of your lives.

If your spouse does not agree to go through the book with you, you can still use the book to enrich your marriage. You can tell your partner what you are learning and ask some of the discussion questions casually, rather than hoping that your partner will read the topic and be familiar with it. Read each chapter completely and record in your journal your answers to the discussions. You will need to arrange time with your spouse regularly when you will not be distracted, such as having dinner alone without the children, meeting after the children are in bed, or taking walks alone. When you have your spouse's attention, tell him or her one thing you wrote in your journal and ask one of the discussion questions. For example, in chapter 1, Exercise 1 suggests writing a list of roles you play. If you are a wife you can say, "One of my roles right now is being a mother of two little children. I want to tell you how I describe myself." Tell your husband your three adjectives. Tell him your feelings about your role. Ask him, "How do you describe yourself as a father?" "How do you feel about your role?" If you have a different opinion from your partner, do not discredit his or her opinion. Hear it out completely before expressing your own. The next time you are walking together, you might say, "Another role I play is daughter. I want to tell you what kind of daughter I am and how I feel about it." And then ask, "Tell me about another role you play. How do you feel about it?"

Do not hurry through the chapters. You may have time for only one question in your first conversation. It may take many months to discuss all the topics, questions, and exercises in *Recreating Marriage*, but getting to know each other is a long-range project that lasts all your married life. You can talk together on car trips, while waiting in the airport, or at the beach. However, if your partner does not want to talk about a particular question, respect his or her need for privacy about the topic or the need not to be in conversation at the moment.

PART I.
Identity—Here I Am

The LORD called Samuel again. . . . And he got up . . . and said, "Here I am, for you called me."

—1 Sam. 3:8

The way to begin a happy marriage is for each partner to recognize the value of the other. Each person is called to a special purpose in life. That purpose, our "call," is to be ourselves, as vigorously and boldly as possible, contributing our talents, temperament, and experiences to our family and community, and thus fulfilling the promise we were born with. Love is nurturing and promoting your spouse's fullest expression of humanity, and living out your own call at the same time. It is not easy.

Giving and receiving love is one of the most pleasurable and important aspects of life. When we feel loved, we are blessed. We rise to our fullest potential. Without it we wither. But something happens after we are married to dampen and mute love, unless we know how to nourish it. Loving a husband or wife requires the full expression of our being. We must open ourselves in order to be intimate, a task requiring intention and courage. Shame and doubts about ourselves get in the way. To be fully loving, we must know that we are worthy of love. Feeling lovable requires a relationship with God and a spiritual journey.

In chapter 1, you will learn about the three aspects of love: romantic love, loving feelings, and loving commitment. Spontaneous, overwhelming, romantic love is relatively short-lived in a marriage, but those feelings can be recalled intentionally by symbolic activities that put you in a romantic mood. Loving feelings replace romantic love in a marriage. This love is more substantial and lasting. Loving feelings create a bond that comes from expressing yourself fully and being received. Loving commitment is determination to nurture and support one's partner, regardless of feelings. Loving actions, which express loving feelings and commitment, are necessary for a partner to feel loved. Many people have misconceptions about loving actions; as a result of those misconceptions, they stifle loving feelings.

In chapter 2 you will learn that your identity is a powerful influence in your life and your marriage. Your identity is who you are as God sees you, the best part of you that is created in God's image and carries God's spirit. Your identity is not what you think or feel about yourself, but who you really are, which you cannot ever know completely. Nonetheless, part 1 will help you and your spouse recognize some aspects of your identities and affirm each other, bringing out the best in each person. For a marriage to be joyful, intimate, and harmonious, both partners must have the opportunity for self-expression. We feel in love when we are recognized and valued.

Our identity determines much of our behavior. It is a combination of the personality traits we were born with and all the experiences that shaped us, particularly our early family life. Being male or female also makes up an important aspect of our identity. As we mature, we should evaluate the identity we were given by our family and take responsibility for developing ourselves.

Another way to understand yourself and your spouse is through the lens of the Myers-Briggs personality framework, simple categories of preferences and temperaments that describe how people behave. The Myers-Briggs personality framework provides couples with a language for describing each other's behavior respectfully. Couples can view problems in terms of personality type rather than regarding each other's behavior as a personal affront. In chapter 3 you'll learn that all personalities are positive. Yes, yours and your spouse's! Preferences are patterns of behavior that you choose over and over because you enjoy them. You will learn that there are four pairs of preferences with each of them having their own distinct features.

Chapter 4 covers the four temperaments, which are a combination of preferences, in order to deepen an appreciation of personalities. You will learn to recognize your strengths and learn how weaknesses are actually a strength carried to an extreme that needs some balance.

Chapter 5 addresses how to live with differences in preferences and temperaments. Many conflicts arise because partners do not understand the differences in their personalities and do not know what to do about those differences. You will learn how to appreciate your differences, make them valuable resources instead of problems, and learn to strengthen weaknesses in your marriage.

Chapter One

The Gift of Love

This chapter will help you understand what to expect from love and encourage you to express your love in a variety of ways. You will learn how to feel worthy of being loved, which is necessary to give and receive love.

What Is Love?

Love binds two people together, as gravity attracts objects to each other, as God's love binds us to God. It focuses our attention on our partner. We know instinctively how close or distant our partner is and we respond to that space with pleasure or anxiety. When we say, "I love you," usually we are referring to the emotional pleasure or sexual attraction we experience when we think of our spouse. People want these pleasurable feelings of love in their relationships, but there is much confusion about how to sustain love. Often people think love is "chemistry," something you have or you don't. Most people feel something in the early months or years of their relationship that they think is love. But as years pass, something happens to those early feelings.

Love is a gift from God. You cannot make yourself feel love or make another person love you, just as you cannot create your own heartbeat. Loving feelings grow and flourish naturally in the presence of certain conditions, in the presence of loving behavior. To behave in a way that nurtures love, you must feel worthy of giving and receiving love.

Most people have experienced love, because it is a powerful and common human emotion. Being in love delights us and its absence strikes us in our most vulnerable place, where we can feel most hurt. But we all have our own unique experience and definition of love. When you say, "I love you," to your spouse, what do you mean? Do you think your partner knows what you mean? And yet, clear or not, those words are very important to hear. If a spouse says, "I don't love you any more," we are devastated before even asking what that means.

It is not unusual for loving feelings to be covered over by hurt, anger, resentment, or fear. At such times, love feels dead or absent. Conflicts are the result of natural differences between partners, but most people do not know how to handle conflicts well. Painful emotions or deadness to love is a sign of partners handling conflicts poorly. Hurt, anger, resentment, or fear can last for years if not dealt with. When you feel other intense emotions, you will not feel love at the same time. The unpleasant emotion must be attended to properly so that healing occurs, which allows the flow of loving feelings again. Most often, love only feels dead, but is waiting, ready to come to life with the hope that conflicts can be resolved. Recreating Marriage educates couples and gives them the skills to manage conflict so that loving feelings can flow.

Discussion 1 will help you put your feelings into words, so that you can express your love more clearly and openly. The questions help you explore your feelings, so there are no "right answers." Answer the questions before reading further.

DISCUSSION 1. *What is love to you? How does love feel? Write the answers to those questions in your journal, and tell your partner about what you wrote. If writing seems unnecessary, you can skip that step.*

Philosophers, theologians, and poets have attempted to define love for centuries. Although many definitions can apply, the three aspects of love I discuss below are the ones I find most helpful to couples who are trying to enhance their relationship. These aspects are love as a romantic dream, love as feelings of intimacy, and loving commitment. These distinctions are useful because you can enhance love in your relationship by focusing on a specific aspect. If you are missing love in one aspect, there is something specific to talk about and work on. Each experience of love can be present in a marriage without the other, but marriages feel most rewarding if intimacy and loving commitment are both present and partners' actions express that.

Love as a Romantic Dream

We experience romantic love when we "fall in love." It usually produces sexual feelings, thrill, and excitement connected with being with the loved person. This kind of love is the popular inspiration of songs, film, and literature. It is a pleasurable experience because you believe the person you love is your romantic ideal, will remove all the obstacles facing you, and give you the life of your dreams. Romantic love emanates from the idealization of the other person. It is a hypnotic state of mind in which positive aspects of the beloved person are affirmed and negative aspects are denied. Romantic love is an illusion, but it is fun. Most of us remember the early days of courtship and marriage and wish we felt that way again.

This kind of love can feel wonderful or miserable, depending on whether loving feelings and loving behavior are also part of your relationship. When we remember being in love, we usually recall the delight, not the agonizing hours worrying about if or when we would be together again. Or the terror we felt if we knew our beloved was on a date with someone else.

Romantic love changes after you have been married for a while. Real life intrudes on the dream of the ideal. Romantic love is usually transformed in the process of living together into intimacy or committed action. Nonetheless, you can rekindle the memories and cultivate the experience of romantic love. It will be a conscious act rather than the overwhelming desire you felt during the beginning of your new life together, but you can nurture romance by symbolic gestures that remind you of romantic feelings. Some common gestures in our culture are sending flowers, cards, candy, and presents; leaving loving notes in unexpected places; having dinner by candlelight; taking simple camping trips or exotic vacations; or simply visiting the familiar old haunts that bring back memories.

DISCUSSION 2. *Write a list of the symbolic gestures of romance you and your partner used during the romantic stage of your marriage. Share your list with your spouse. Think of one new romantic symbol to surprise your spouse with in the future.*

DISCUSSION 3. *Tell each other about an occasion when you were aware of romantic love for your partner. Tell your partner if you have noticed a change in the "in love" feeling in your relationship and when that change occurred. What feelings replaced the "in love" feeling?*

Love as a Feeling of Intimacy

Love as intimacy feels like an open heart. Your chest feels warm; your breathing deep; you feel pleasure in the presence of the other. You feel connection and belonging. It is being touched by someone and touching that person at the level of the soul, being transparent, without filters or defenses. This love relates to the essence of a person. At the time you experience love, you suspend evaluations to allow yourself to be fully attentive to another. This kind of love requires vulnerability. It is the fuel of well-being and allows you to enjoy the relationship and life in general. In a good marriage, this love grows deeper with passing time. It is more substantial and lasting than romantic love.

Our awareness of this kind of love ebbs and flows, moment to moment, depending on what is happening in our lives. It is more likely to be felt in tender and special moments. When we are at work concentrating on getting a project done on time, we do not experience love, although we may remind ourselves of that feeling when we look at our partner's photo on the desk.

People can feel a deep sense of intimacy with persons other than their spouse, such as a parent, sibling, or good friend. Intimacy will then have a different context, of course, because the experiences shared will be different. Although sharing with other people can be profound, no other relationship has the ongoing mutual dependency and vulnerability of that with a spouse. Intimacy with a spouse includes sharing sexual experiences, sharing major events such as having babies together and nurturing those children through their stages of development, sharing in routines of survival such as creating income and preparing food, and being each other's primary caregiver during illness.

Some people never felt romantic love for their partners but, instead, have feelings of intimacy. Either kind of love can nurture a relationship if the partners *believe* it can. If one partner does not feel romantic love and the other sees this as a problem, then the partners will be dissatisfied.

Kevin and Jan, a client couple, felt love for each other and had a relationship that satisfied both of them in many ways. However, Jan did not feel the intense romantic love she had once experienced for another man and was hesitant to marry Kevin without it. She had to put into perspective how important romantic love was to her before she could appreciate the love she had for Kevin. Kevin, in the meantime, alternated between understanding and worry. He felt nothing was missing from their relationship because Jan was very tender, affectionate, and sexually responsive, but he was concerned that she would be unhappy about the absence of those overwhelming romantic feelings. Through many conversations about love and from sharing intimate experiences Jan came to appreciate the kind of love she shared with Kevin.

Some people think erroneously that "If my partner loved me," she or he would (you name it—make love with enthusiasm, help with housework, listen to me). Tender, intimate feeling can, but does not necessarily, lead to loving behavior. People can feel love and not treat their partner well, because of ineffective beliefs about themselves, their relationship, and their marriage. These ineffective beliefs were usually formed in childhood as they saw family members in action. A young man may have learned to be dominating and argumentative like his father, for example. He may never have learned to give affirmations and appreciation. He may feel love for his wife, but not know how to act so she receives it. But this can change.

DISCUSSION 4. *Tell your partner about an occasion when you were aware of feeling intimate love for him or her. Describe in detail what was happening when you felt loving and close.*

Love as a Commitment to the Other's Well-Being

A happy marriage needs a mixture of intimate feelings and loving commitment. Loving commitment is determination and resolve that the loved person should flourish. This love is more than a decision or a promise. Loving commitment is an act of will. It is taking a stand for what shall be. This love calls forth persistence and courage that can seem heroic when circumstances require it. On a daily basis this commitment motivates spouses to consider the other person before taking action.

Loving commitment can come forth from romantic love or intimacy. Often romantic love is the inspiration for commitment. In the midst of romantic love, partners may pledge to love each other forever. Or as a result of the sweetness of intimacy, partners may commit to spending their lives together. But loving commitment must reach beyond loving feelings or it is not commitment. Feelings are emotions that come and go with circumstances. Loving commitment can endure when feelings are not there.

Loving commitment does not feel like warm, open, pleasant feelings similar to romantic love or intimacy. It means giving your word about your intention. To give your word that you will be committed to your spouse's well-being you must have three things.

1. Self-knowledge. You need to know your own capabilities. You need to know that you can live happily with another person and make mutual decisions with that person. If you really want to make your own decisions and avoid the intrusion of someone else's wants and needs, you are not equipped for a loving commitment. And you

need to know that you have something to contribute to the relationship as a partner; that you will be a support and not a burden to the other person.

2. Self-confidence. You need self-confidence because often you will not know what to do. Still, you need the confidence that you will figure it out when the time comes.

3. Courage. Some circumstances will be overwhelming and you will not know what to do. It takes courage to keep persisting in the face of the odds.

Commitment to another person's well-being must supersede commitment to the endurance of the marriage. Often people think they are committed to their partner, but their real commitment is to holding on to the marriage. Sincere commitment to a partner means talking with your spouse with an open mind to hear what will benefit him or her. Many of my clients have tried to persuade their spouses to do what they thought would keep the partner tied to the marriage: urging spouses to have sex with them, limiting their spouses' friendships, urging spouses not to work outside the home, discouraging spouses from going out of town without them, or, finally, persuading spouses that the children would be damaged if the spouses did not comply. These clients present themselves as committed to the marriage, claiming their spouses are not. The paradox is that when a partner is committed to the *spouse*, rather than committed to keeping the marriage together, the spouse usually responds by wanting to stay in the marriage.

Marla attends to her husband, Neil, rather than holding on to her marriage. Neil had an affair, which hurt Marla deeply. In therapy, Marla recognized that neither she nor Neil knew how to talk about difficult subjects in their marriage. She had not openly expressed her feelings, and this, combined with critical comments, had not been pleasant for Neil. She was determined to change. Neil moved out so that he could sort out his confusion about the marriage. Marla told him she loved him and was committed to him. She feared that Neil would return to his affair. But her deepest commitment was to Neil's well-being. She helped Neil move to an old house that he bought. She encouraged and helped him to visit their young son. He appreciated that she supported his separation. After a month, Neil began inviting Marla for dates. They started having frequent conversations. Marla was at times tempted to criticize Neil, but talked about her feelings instead. It was difficult for her to change. She did not know whether Neil would recognize the change and come home. As they gradually did more things together, Neil began to trust that he could talk with Marla openly. Intimacy developed that they had never had before. After a year, Neil returned home.

DISCUSSION 5. *Recall when you first gave your commitment to be in a loving relationship with your partner. The occasion may have been the same for each of you or a different one. Tell your partner about what you remember.*

DISCUSSION 6. *Identify a time when you used persistence and courage as a result of your loving commitment. Tell your partner about this occasion.*

Loving Actions Benefit the Beloved

Both intimacy and commitment are nurtured by loving behavior. Loving feelings benefit only the person who loves. Your spouse does not benefit from your feelings. Your spouse benefits only from your behavior. Ultimately, the well-being of your marriage will depend on what you do, not on what you feel. The problem for many people is that they do not know what actions are loving. Yes, loving action means doing helpful things for each other that we do not object to doing, such as helping each other with chores, remembering birthdays and anniversaries, and telling your partner what you appreciate. But some people believe that loving actions are doing whatever your spouse requests and not denying the person anything. They think an act of love is withholding negative feelings—complaints, resentment, sadness, loneliness, and anger. These are misconceptions. If a spouse acts on these beliefs over the years, intimacy will be eroded because there is no honest expression of emotions.

Acts of love include fully expressing yourself and encouraging self-expression from your partner, because self-expression maintains intimacy. You are as committed to your partner's life being satisfying and meaningful as you are your own. It means cultivating activities that both of you enjoy doing together. It means being honest about problems and trying to solve them in a mutually agreeable way. It moves you to tell your spouse what is important to you even if you know it will temporarily cause conflict, and to listen with equal interest. It is making a request when you feel like being critical and demeaning. Loving action motivates you to keep or renegotiate your promises when you don't feel like doing so. In short, as you will see, it is Recreating Marriage.

Behaving in a loving way does not imply that you feel loving at the time. Often you will do something that benefits your partner because you are committed to the well-being of that person and the marriage. Loving actions are the many things you do to please your spouse, such as arranging for the baby-sitter to come on Saturdays, honoring birthdays, making special meals, leaving a friendly message on the voice mail, or fulfilling a request. You may not be feeling love at the time you do it. In fact, loving action may make us uncomfortable at times, such as when we do things we do not enjoy because of love for someone else. For example, I listen to Nate when he needs me to, even if I am feeling angry. I am not feeling loving at the time, but listening is a loving act that benefits Nate. And I know that after I listen to Nate, he will listen to me.

Loving feelings will not last long without loving action. After all, loving feelings benefit only the person who has the feeling. It is your *behavior* that benefits your partner. If you feel love for your husband, for example, but never make time for conversations and pleasant events, and never accept his requests, he will not experience your love, no matter how much you say, "I love you."

DISCUSSION 7. *Tell your spouse about something you did because you love him or her. Ask whether he or she knew that you were expressing love by your deed. Your spouse may not know when you feel love unless you say so.*

✔ **EXERCISE 1.**
Ask your spouse to make a list of the things you could do to make her or him feel loved, and make a list of your own. Share your lists.

DISCUSSION 8. *Write the answer to this question in your journal, and share the answer with your spouse: How do you know when your partner loves you?*

Love and Change

Loving for a lifetime requires being able to change together. Change is inevitable as you go through the experiences of life—having children, establishing family routines, relating to each others' parents, living through illnesses and deaths, coping with teenagers, changing jobs or locations, and creating a life alone after children leave. These life experiences create opportunities to enrich your marriage and strengthen your partnership. Some couples who have been married for many years say that they have had several marriages—to the same person. Through Recreating Marriage you are learning how to create the possibility for a lasting love.

When we get married we open ourselves to another person. That opening can feel like destruction or creation, and usually both are occurring. When our identity is challenged by anyone, including our spouse, we experience negative emotions such as anger, resentment, frustration, and sadness. When our identity is supported, we experience competence, pleasure, belonging, and joy. To maintain intimacy and understanding over a lifetime, couples must communicate effectively about the changes they are going through. Emotions reflect like a mirror the flow of breaking down and building up of identity. We are not objects fixed in time. We are in a constant process of becoming, like a river. The river has a geographical location, but the water in that river is constantly changing. If you are not communicating, you could be living with a stranger. Your partner seems on the outside to be the recognizable person you know, and yet the flow of emotional experiences is constantly occurring within that person, tearing down and building up, changing the person internally.

This tearing down and building up of each partner's identity is not always pleasant for either person. In fact, it can be painful. Love makes us willing to go through the hard times when it would be easier to give up. In a good marriage both people change. The change is not just a compromise, with both people giving up part of themselves to make way for the other person. Instead, it is a true integration of differences.

For example, I normally approach life negatively. For me, life is a whole bunch of problems to solve or worry about. I try to keep my world small enough so I can manage the problems within it. I am an excellent problem solver, but sometimes I get overwhelmed by the sheer amount I require of myself. Nate's belief about life is very different. He experiences life as holding an infinite variety of opportunities. If things are going badly today, he believes an exciting experience is just around the corner.

I unwittingly came to rely on Nate's optimism. I noticed he created opportunities that I would never have considered. He takes risks that make life more interesting. When he worked out of town and left me alone several days a week, I noticed my pessimistic thoughts surfaced in clear contrast to Nate's promising ideas. I worried that I would not have enough money, that housing in my neighborhood would lose its value, that the schools were not adequate, that my daughter would marry the wrong person. I was angry with Nate for leaving all the problems for me to handle. I complained, to no avail.

My anger could have interfered with our love. It didn't, because I took on the project of changing my pessimistic thinking by changing my beliefs, one at a time. Particularly useful was finding other people who thought positively about the things that bothered me. I talked with friends about how they budget money. I attended community meetings to discuss the schools. I even went to city hall and found an official who could give me information and reassurance. Noticing what is working gives me lightness of heart and step when Nate is not around. I do not want to give up my ability to see problems and therefore to solve them, but my awareness has been forever expanded.

For Nate's part, he had a habit of avoiding problems. Although he may not like my pointing out the flaws in his "best-laid plans," he recognized that I make things really work. I can turn a wish into a reality by solving all the problems to get there. We make a good combination. Through the years, Nate has been able to recognize and grapple with obstacles more effectively as a result of living with me. Both of us experienced a profound change that is integrated into our identity.

DISCUSSION 9. *Tell your spouse one way in which you have changed since you met.*

Am I Lovable?

In order to give and receive love, you need to believe that you are lovable. You must be willing to be open to being vulnerable, the real you. If you feel ashamed or unworthy of love, you will not allow your partner to see you. You will hold back and not express yourself. Your shame will get in the way of intimacy.

Believing you are lovable is one of the most powerful beliefs affecting your relationship. Loving yourself contributes to loving another person because when you love yourself, you do not depend on your spouse to build you up. You do not need your spouse to prove it by constantly demonstrating his or her feelings. Your partner is free to express love in his or her own time and way. Then you can freely ask for what you want (such as a hug, a back rub, or to share making meals) without the request implying that your spouse would already be doing it if you were lovable. You would never interpret your spouse's behavior as an indication of your worth.

"Am I a loving and lovable person?" is one of the ultimate questions that we ask ourselves. Ultimate questions such as, "What is my life's purpose?" and "What is my relationship to God?" are at the center of our identity. The question, "Am I loving and lovable?" is central to our "self-talk," our internal dialog. Too often, when we marry, we expect our spouse to counteract our negative feelings about ourselves or to disprove our sense of inferiority or unlovability. We imbue this poor person who married us with the power to answer the ultimate question about our own worth. We ask so much of our spouse that the job is impossible. Disappointment and hurt are inevitable. No wonder many of my clients say, "I can get along well with everyone but my spouse." When we confer the power to determine whether we are lovable on our partner, it should not be surprising that we eventually feel resentment. To experience freedom and joy in a relationship, it is necessary to assume the responsibility for our own self-definition and to liberate our spouse from that responsibility.

Each of us has grown up believing that we are either worthy or unworthy of love. This belief was communicated in a variety of ways to us by our parents and family. A child receives a parent's touch and voice very personally. If the parent's touch is warm and soothing the child feels cared for. Later, the child develops a belief that he or she is *worthy* of care. Some people grew up in families that welcomed their arrival with the fanfare that they deserved; their parents' lives were harmonious, and their parents provided them with the kind of activities that enriched their talents and temperament. They have stories of love to tell. These people are probably unusual. Most of us have some kind of wound that hampers loving.

Children who feel deprived of love may think, "If I were more lovable, my parents would not have divorced." Or, "If I were more lovable, my parents would provide me with better clothes and toys." Or, "If I were more lovable, my parents would not argue about me." Children do not consider that their parents may have problems they are dealing with which causes them to behave in a certain way—to suddenly flare up and criticize a child or, on the other hand, to spend hours enthralling a child with stories. They do not consider that their parents are worried about having enough money, are abusing alcohol, or are unable to express themselves to anyone. As children, we just take it all to mean we are lovable or not.

Children may sacrifice their own identity in order to be loved. They can believe erroneously that they are so lovable that they can rescue their parents from adult problems. Children naturally exaggerate their own power in order to cope with feeling helpless. A child may try to be so lovable that Dad never gets drunk or Mom stops crying. A daughter becomes a father's darling, providing love and comfort that Dad is missing in the world of adults. A son becomes super-responsible to make his mother feel secure. For people who grew up like this, being lovable can be a burden.

It was in the aftermath of the breakdown of my first marriage that I took responsibility for being lovable. As an adult, I know that my parents loved me very much. But I interpreted circumstances and events in my childhood to mean I was not lovable. I was born during World War II, the first child of a father who was in the Navy and a mother who was living away from her home in Mississippi. My father was absent most of my young years, but Mother had the support of her sister some of the time. When I was two, my brother was born. We moved every few years as Dad was transferred. When I was eight years old, Dad became ill with tuberculosis and spent eighteen months hospitalized. After his discharge from the hospital and Navy, we moved to Mississippi, where I lived until I left for graduate school.

I was sad as a child because I was lonely. I was shy and a natural introvert, so I made friends slowly. Before friendships would get very deep, we would move. The first image of myself that I remember is of being different from other kids. I did not fit into the social groups that already existed wherever I went. My parents were struggling for survival in strange towns or on a small farm, and my social needs were not a priority. I mistook their preoccupation with their own lives as a message about my unworthiness. I mistook the natural social boundaries of other children as a message about my undesirability. I mistook the teachings of a small-town fundamentalist church as a message about my sinfulness. I mistook my first husband's neediness as a message about my being lovable. I mistook his leaving me for another woman as a message about my failure as a wife. My identity has undergone many revisions since I began to be aware of myself. During the terrible emotional turmoil of separation I started taking responsibility for who I am instead of accepting how I was defined by other people.

The process of encountering another person intimately forces you to encounter yourself. Who you think you are is eventually exposed by the constant observation and response of your partner. Probably you would not have recognized me twenty years ago as a person whose identity suffered from an onslaught of self-criticism. I looked and functioned like a successful psychologist, but internally, I was depending on men to compensate for my self-rejection.

When my first husband left me I felt intense rage and grief, the most intense negative experience I had lived through. I felt as though my body was no longer anchored by gravity, but was careening off into space. I felt completely alone and ashamed. But as I recovered from the breakdown of a marriage, I examined what I had been doing to myself and my relationship with my husband. As a result of his leaving, I questioned my beliefs about how marriages work. I had to examine my life. I recognized that I had been depressed in that marriage for two years. The ideas I had clung to did not work.

Does this suggest that it was necessary for my husband to leave me in order for me to develop an identity I could claim, for me to express myself fully and live in a way that creates intimacy? I have pondered that question a lot, and will never know if he and I could have matured and had a joyful relationship. I do know that I was forced to learn about life without him, and I have a joyful marriage now with Nate. I stopped looking for a man to tell me I am lovable. I could then experience the man for his own sake. I felt lovable before I met Nate. My feeling lovable gave Nate the freedom to be authentic with me—at various times playful, serious, warm, frustrated, distant, sexual, adventuresome, exuberant—all the ways that Nate can be Nate.

DISCUSSION 10. *Share with your spouse a time in your life in which you did not feel lovable. It may have been only a brief moment or of longer duration.*

DISCUSSION 11. *Tell your spouse about experiences in which you feel most lovable.*

DISCUSSION 12. *Discuss with your spouse how you learned about being lovable.*

Exercise 2, below, introduces a process to change your thinking from believing that you are unlovable to accepting that you are lovable, without your spouse having to prove it. This process allows you to put past experiences in the past and separate them from your present. If you do not feel lovable, this change will take some time. Be patient with yourself.

If you grew up confident that you are lovable, this exercise might help you understand a partner who did not.

✔ **EXERCISE 2.**
   1. **Share with your spouse what was happening in your parents' lives at the time of your birth. What was their financial status? How many children were they caring for when you were born? What was their relationship with their parents?**

2. **As you think about your parents' lives when you were young, how much emotional, financial, and practical support did they have to give you?**

3. **What message did you get from your parents about whether you were a lovable child? How did their own circumstances affect their ability to demonstrate love for you?**

4. **Look at the context of your parents' lives. Separate the past from the present. Update the messages that you received about being lovable. Tell your spouse your new belief about being lovable.**

5. **Discuss with your spouse how believing that you are worthy of love will affect your relationship.**

God's Love

Religion teaches about God's love for us. We all got different messages, depending on how our faith was passed on to us by our pastor, congregation, and family. Some of us learned that God loves us. But some of us learned that God was severely disapproving of us. As adults, we must be able to evaluate our early beliefs about ourselves and learn about God's love from an adult perspective, rather than feel stuck with the definition that was handed to us by someone else.

I invite each of you to know God's love and to declare to yourself that you are lovable. Through God's grace, you are that spark of God that belongs uniquely to you. Your authentic self that is under all the layers of self-defense is made in the image of God, and is fully lovable. As a person with limited perspective and capabilities, you make mistakes. You hurt other people. For all that, you are forgiven over and over again. This may be a new way of saying something that is familiar. Or the idea that you are a reflection of God may feel like a religious conversion. Believing that you are a beloved and forgiven child of God is an antidote for self-degradation and guilt. At least, begin to search for a belief that supports you as a positive expression of humanity.

When you can be in the presence of God-in-you and God-in-your-partner, you will be filled with awe. You will marvel at God's incredible creative power and love. You will be inspired to care for such an extraordinary creature. You will be moved to treat yourself and your spouse (and your children) with respect. You will not choose to hurt these creatures of God with your words, destructive actions, neglect, or chemicals such as alcohol or drugs.

Yet you will feel inadequate to care for yourself and your spouse in the way you wish you could. You are unskilled. Recreating Marriage will help you acquire some skills needed to treat yourself and your spouse as you deserve: as the creatures God made.

To Remember as Time Goes By

1. Loving feelings are a natural response to a person to whom we express our identity openly and from whom we receive affirmation. In other words, we feel vulnerable yet safe.
2. You cannot make yourself feel love.
3. You cannot make someone love you.
4. Loving actions create an opportunity for loving feelings.
5. The potential for a loving bond and intimacy exists for every couple.
6. Acting in a loving way can be a conscious decision.

For Practice

Notice when the three aspects of love are present in your marriage. Tell your partner when you feel loving and loved.

Chapter Two

Identity and Intimacy

In this chapter you will learn (1) that you and your spouse each have an identity that profoundly affects your relationship and (2) some ways of sharing your identities to create intimacy. When you can share your identity with your spouse, and receive your spouse's acceptance, you feel in love and intimate.

Intimacy Is Sharing Who We Are

When we share the unfolding revelation of ourselves with the person we married, we experience the delight of being deeply touched. We feel connected and not alone. A marriage is two people, each with an identity, discovering, revealing, and expressing that identity. Revealing and expressing ourselves to each other creates intimacy—that coveted, elusive treasure we grasp for in marriage. Intimacy is paradoxical; it is such a simple concept, yet so difficult to create. Personal experience provides little preparation for this process.

Family theory developers, Michael E. Kerr, M.D., and Murray Bowen, M.D., suggest that need for intimacy and identity are inherited by virtue of being human.[1] They call intimate love between spouses "the togetherness force," and they refer to identity as a "solid self." Healthy couples regulate intimacy and separateness in a way that balances those needs for both spouses. In Recreating Marriage you will learn some ways to increase intimacy through revealing yourself, listening to your partner without judgment, and appreciating and affirming your partner. You will learn to make requests and promises, which adds to trust and partnership. However, you must have an identity in order to know what you want to request and to make promises that you are willing to keep. As you practice the skills in Recreating Marriage, both your intimacy and your confidence in your own identity will increase.

Everyone wants to be loved for who she or he *really* is. Not just because she is the mother of your children, she gives you sex, she cooks dinner, and she keeps the house. Not just because he makes the money, takes care of the cars and yard, and goes to movies and dinner with you. As a therapist, I have found that a satisfying marriage supports the identities of both persons in the couple. People who feel their identities are supported within their marriages love their partners and love their lives. People who feel their identities are not supported either leave the marriage or remain miserable within it.

Self-revelation. What's so hard about that? While hearing good things about ourselves is sweet, being criticized or disregarded is painful. Saying and doing anything exposes us to criticism, but when we express something that is full of personal meaning and emotion, criticism in response can hurt much more. As a result, we might not take the chance of revealing ourselves in order to avoid the pain.

Identity Is a Gift of God

It is not easy to say who we are, even if we have the courage to do so, because identity is an elusive concept. Our identity separates us from everyone else in the universe, just as our physical skin separates our physical bodies from the rest of the world. Our identity is contained in the boundary between "me" and "not me."

We never know who we really are. Only God knows us that thoroughly. Our identity is the part of us that God has made whole, good, and lovable. Your identity is the totality of your potential. Some aspects of your identity are manifest in your values, beliefs, preferences, roles, talents, and capabilities. All we can have is our perception or belief about who we are. However, there are ways of illuminating our identity. For example, when we speak the truth, we reveal our identity. When we take a stand for something important, our values and beliefs, we expose ourselves. The roles we play and how we feel about them inform us about our identity. Emotions are evidence that something deep inside has been touched. Your identity is the spiritual part of you that is responsible for making all components of yourself work together. Your identity is the chooser, rather than the choice. To use James Hillman's metaphor, our identity is the acorn, the defining image, out of which an oak grows.[2]

Identity is that spark of divine light, truth, God, or way of being that belongs uniquely to each of us. No two identities are the same. Identity is the authentic self that is under all the layers of pretense. Lecturer, writer, and former Catholic monk Thomas Moore uses the word "soul" to mean the genuine and deep part of us.[3]

In Luke 17:21 Jesus says, "the kingdom of God is within you." The most positive identity we can affirm is that each of us is an expression of God. Theologian and Trappist monk Thomas Merton affirms the potential of

people as an expression of God.[4] For Merton, God wants us to be ourselves clearly and vigorously. To be ourselves is to praise our Creator.
Excitement, joy, and vitality occur when our behavior matches who we
are, or our identity. It is called "alignment" when all parts of our lives are
in agreement, as all the wheels of a car go in the same direction when the
wheels are aligned. There is no need for a pretense or mask.

Knowing who we are, accepting ourselves, and expressing ourselves
is a lifelong process of discovery and refinement, a spiritual journey.
People can be self-centered and destructive when they are unaware of
God's presence and have no knowledge of God's spirit in them. This may
happen when a person has grown up abused, neglected, and unloved.
Instead of being a vessel of God's light, that person's identity is smoth-
ered with hate. Still, anyone can know God and know her or his true
identity. Each person comes to God in a different and special way.
Everyone's call is personal.

Growth in a marriage is interwoven with spiritual growth. Marriage
confronts you with parts of yourself you would rather not see. Through
encountering your beloved partner and dealing with your issues, you
come closer to being the person you were born to be.

> Iron sharpens iron,
>   and one person sharpens the wits of another. . . .
> Just as water reflects the face,
>   so one human heart reflects another.
>
> Prov. 27:17–19

In the journey of discovery, you come face to face with yourself, as
well as your partner. For example, if part of you is a curious adventurer,
spend some time in discovery of the world. If part of you is a neglectful
housekeeper, accept that part of yourself also. You can accept yourself
and also work on what you would like to change. When you accept that
beneath your flaws is a competent and loving person, change is much
easier than when you berate yourself for being insufficient, inadequate,
and unlovable. Being at peace with yourself releases love, health, and
vitality. Although you will still have conflicts with your spouse, you will
be a more receptive listener. However, even when your behavior and
identity are somewhat consistent, life will not always be pleasant. When
you are being yourself, you will feel the full range of human emotion,
including frustration, sadness, joy, anger, and love.

Self-esteem is a word used to describe how we feel about our identity
or ourselves. People often have a single-perspective judgment about

themselves, mostly noticed when that judgment is negative. Sometimes my clients will say, "I have a problem with low self-esteem." They mean they are not the person they want to be. Most people feel this from time to time. We reject ourselves without considering that we have admirable qualities along with the flaws. I use *identity* instead of *self-esteem* because people have many dimensions. Some aspects of yourself you may like and others you may not. Identity gives you a way of thinking about many aspects of yourself.

Personality is a word used by psychologists to describe someone. Personality means all patterns of a person's behavior, including negative and destructive behavior. Your personality is what other people experience when they encounter you. Your personality does not say who you are on the inside, but only what comes through externally. Internal identity may be more positive than external personality if a person does not know how to behave in a way that gets intended results. People with destructive and evil personalities are not revering themselves and others as creatures of God, and they are unskilled in constructive ways to meet their needs.

How Is Identity Revealed?

We know ourselves and each other through our perceptions and the meaning we attribute to those perceptions. Our insight and knowledge are always partial. Therefore, we should approach discovery of ourselves and each other with an open mind and humility. The process I present for understanding yourself and others is a way to affirm yourself, use your strengths in your marriage, and minimize and balance the weaknesses. However, this process is only one lens by which to view yourself.

We know ourselves and each other by verbal and nonverbal patterns of thoughts, feelings, and behavior that distinguish us. These distinguishing patterns are preferences, values, beliefs, roles, and emotions. The following discussion introduces you to these patterns. They are discussed thoroughly in subsequent chapters.

Preferences

A *preference* is a way of behaving that you choose over and over. It almost goes without saying that we enjoy our preferences and they are a natural part of us. Preferences determine whether your energy comes more from inside you or the world outside yourself, whether you like mental activities or physical activities, whether you are a rational problem solver or a people-oriented problem solver, and whether you like to plan or be spontaneous. I describe four pairs of preferences in chapters 3 and 4.

In a happy marriage, each person's style should be appreciated. But, instead, preferences are often a source of conflict. Most couples do not know how to handle their differences in preferences. In chapters 3, 4, and 5 you will learn how to use preferences to better understand yourself and your spouse, and learn tools that will enable you to work out differences.

Values and Beliefs

Values and *beliefs* motivate and guide our decisions. They are the channels through which our identity is expressed. Values are categories of experiences. Values are derived from experiences that bring us joy, happiness, fulfillment, self-respect, and pleasure. Examples of values are achievement, beauty, competition, education, family, integrity, pleasure, and truth. Each individual is called to a different combination of values. You can recognize a value by how positively or negatively you feel about something. Worth is determined by your emotional response to an experience. If an experience has great appeal to you, it is of great value. Everything you come in contact with and every activity has an emotional value range, from no value to great or priceless value. If you feel negatively about something, that thing may be in direct opposition to an important value. I place great value on my children's health, for example. Anything that interferes with my children's health bothers me and causes me to take action to solve the problem.

Beliefs are what we hold to be true, our perception of reality. But only God knows completely what is real and true. Beliefs have a powerful effect on our lives and marriages. Beliefs provide meaning for our experience because we organize our lives around what we hold to be true. Many of our beliefs are easily identified. We are accustomed to talking about them, although most of us are not aware that it is beliefs we are communicating. Statements involving personal observation and judgment contain beliefs. For example, I believe Nate is in the bedroom because I hear his voice coming from there. Some beliefs are not based on evidence. Belief without observable evidence is faith. Any statement beginning with, "I think . . ." usually identifies a belief.

We choose the values and beliefs by which we live, although during our childhood they are chosen for us. As we grow, our values and beliefs change—but not through persuasion from our spouse. They change from our experience and reflection. We argue and protect our values and beliefs as though we were protecting our lives, even when the person we are arguing with is a spouse who loves us. Differences in values and beliefs are a source of much marital conflict. Communicating clearly about the differences, as you will learn in part 2, is one way of resolving conflicts.

Roles

From your preferences, values, and beliefs, you develop roles. Your roles reflect your identity because you assume them for particular contexts in your life, such as mother, father, wife, gardener, golfer, engineer, or manager. Although many people play the same roles, you play your roles in a way that is unique to you. For example, one of my roles is "Mother with an Empty Nest." Many of my life experiences these days center on having been deeply connected to caring for my children who are no longer present. My feelings have ranged from deep sadness in the thundering silence of children's absence to the joy of returning home in the evening to no one for whom I have to be responsible. Some of my thoughts have been worry about my daughter Ariana's ability to eat a healthy diet in Indonesia, wondering how Jon, my stepson, is getting along in his college classes, and anticipating stepson Dylan's visit in the next week. Sometimes I cry. I write and telephone my three grown children. I make brownies and ship them to Jon. I plan the weekend visit with Dylan.

There are many parts to each person's identity. Some of these parts get along well and some may be in conflict. When my children were younger, the part of me that wanted to be "Nurturing Mother" got in the way of "Ambitious Psychologist." All of us have internal conflicts to manage in order to keep life in balance. In Exercise 1, below, you will look at the roles you play. You may notice your tendency to judge yourself as you describe yourself. This is natural. Try to suspend your judgment and accept whatever comes, even if some descriptions seem negative. If you feel comfortable doing so, share your identity descriptions with your spouse. You may also notice a tendency to judge your spouse's identity. This is not the time for criticism. It is an opportunity for you and your spouse to be accepted for who you say you are.

✔ **EXERCISE 1.**

Think of some of the roles you play. In your journal write three roles. Nate's examples were (1) man, (2) consultant, (3) athlete.

Next, add adjectives to these roles to describe your own special way of creating that role. The role plus the adjectives should come close to describing *part* of your identity. Nate's were the following:

1. Supportive, distracted, family man.

2. Helpful, encouraging, business consultant.

3. Strong, competitive, inactive athlete. (He thinks of himself as an athlete, but he is not participating in any sport now.)

Now, create your own list. Share it with your spouse.

Emotions

Emotions are a signal about whether we are expressing our identity in our lives. Your feelings are not you, but rather an indicator about you, just as your blood pressure is not you, but a signal about your health. If you live with roles, values, beliefs, and preferences that reflect your identity, you are happy. When your behavior is in conflict with your identity, values, or beliefs, you may become depressed or frustrated. Your unhappiness will eventually cause problems in your marriage. You will not be pleasant to live with. You may become withdrawn or critical of others. Sometimes living a life that is not satisfying leads to affairs. A spouse may feel deeply supported by someone else rather than by the person to whom she or he is married. A dangerous result of not living in a way that is right for you is that it may affect your immune system, making you vulnerable to disease. The mind has a powerful effect on the body. In fact, it has been shown that in many cases healing of serious illnesses occurred when patients changed their lives.[5]

Most of us have qualities we do not like. You can develop the skill to change or accept the parts of yourself that bother you. You can also discover parts of your identity that you do like. In Exercise 2, below, you will notice your feelings about the roles you mentioned. Some of your feelings will be pleasant, but some will not. Your feelings indicate how well your roles match your identity. Because we are always changing and because we must live with other people, we can never fulfill ourselves 100 percent. Refining and fine-tuning our roles is part of our spiritual journey.

Nate's comments (see Exercise 2) show he feels frustrated about being away from his family. In the five years since Nate wrote this, he has reduced his out-of-town business and is much happier. Nate gave up competitive sports many years ago and went to graduate school. He misses sports but does not choose to change that role. Nate tells me a lot about his baseball, basketball, and football experiences. Sharing feelings with your spouse about your journey creates intimacy.

✔ **EXERCISE 2.**
In your journal, jot down your feelings about each role you listed

in Exercise 1. You don't need complete sentences. Here are Nate's journal entries:

1. Supportive, distracted, family man. Conflicted between serving needs of clients and family members. Frustrated, not available to support family activities. Unappreciated by family. Tense, anxious, responsible. Overloaded. Important. Enthusiastic about accomplishments of family members.

2. Helpful, encouraging, business consultant. Excitement from high-stakes involvement. Pressured to perform flawlessly. Energized by clients' issues/problems. Adventuresome in quest for new horizons. Appreciated for my talents, abilities, and character. Rich from the process. Vulnerable from being "on the line."

3. Strong, competitive, inactive athlete. Frustrated that there isn't enough time and energy to engage in competitive sports. Relieved that I don't have to make a living as a competitive athlete. Feel like a spectator more than a participant. Miss the intensity and adulation of competition.

Share your journal entries with your spouse. Do not be critical of your feelings. They are indicators of where you need to fine-tune your roles so that you can be more satisfied in the future. You may recognize some conflicts with your spouse's roles. You will learn how to handle these differences.

Where Does Identity Come From?

Some circumstances that affect identity are inherited and some are handed to us by our parents and culture. However, our circumstances do not determine who we are. They only influence us. We respond in our own unique and special way to each one. Four circumstances are important in determining our identity: physical inheritance, family of origin, gender, and life experiences.

Physical Inheritance

Our physical makeup determines, in part, our identity. Our bodies are programmed through millions of years of evolution to respond in ways that are specific to the human organism and to the particular individual. At birth God's wisdom is expressed in our genetic coding, giving us the potential to benefit ourselves and the people around us. We are a particular gender and size, and we have inherited talents and a particular temperament. We have tendencies from birth for certain behaviors. Some of us are bold and adventurous while others are quiet and reflective. Some of us have musical talents while others are good listeners. Our natural personality is modified by life experiences. People are happiest when their environment provides the kind of stimulation in which their individuality can flourish.

Family of Origin

Our family of origin can nurture us to flourish and develop to our full potential or it can stifle and damage us. Our identity is first bestowed on us by our parents. We are the embodiment of their hopes, dreams, fears, and images of themselves. They said "Good boy!" or "Sweetie pie" or "You lazy kid" or worse. They rewarded us for successes, discouraged and criticized us, expected too much or too little, or ignored us. Carl Rogers, one of the founders of modern psychotherapy, calls these events "self-experience," out of which our "concept of self" grows.[6]

As we grew older we separated ourselves from our parents' perceptions of us. As adults, we can evaluate what our parents believed about us, accept what fits, and discard those aspects that are not right for us. We continue to shape our own identity. We long to be somebody significant and to be recognized for our special traits. We want to be cherished by our mate because we are different and distinct in his or her life. Yet we cannot depend on our marital partner to define us. Nor our parents, friends, or bosses. The irony is that we must project to our spouse who we really are. To be defined by someone else is to be stifled, deprived of our own creation.

Gender Identity

We cannot separate ourselves as a person from our gender. Our lives have been shaped by our family's and our culture's response to our gender. We have feelings about our maleness or femaleness. In spite of attempts to provide equal opportunities for boys and girls, they have different life experiences. Girls' play is more gentle and verbally sophisticated, while boys' play is more aggressive and physically active. Parents relate differently to boys and girls. Mothers tend to talk more with girls and touch them more. Boys get more physical discipline.[7] Some families appreciate the intellect of all their children, while others value intellect in one gender more than the other. Some families are gentle and protective of daughters and harsh and demanding of sons. Even in this age of tolerance for the varieties of expression of gender, some families may find it intolerable for a boy to be quiet and sensitive or a girl to be outspoken.

We also learn gender identity from the example of our parents' lives. Normally, as we grow up, we sort out what parts of our parents' behavior we value and want to emulate, and what we want to avoid. We are never oblivious to our parents' strengths and weaknesses—or to the responses of others to them. Boys decide whether they want to be like their fathers, depending on how much they admire and respect them. If a son hears a lot of criticism about his father from his mother and sisters, he may conclude that men are not valued and respected. He will not look forward to growing up to be a man. Likewise, if Mom seems weak and ineffective, a girl may not want to be like her.

It takes time and soul searching to separate ourselves from our parents' definitions of men and women and to create definitions of our own. We carry our impressions of our gender into our marriage, with pride about being male or female, or shame and fear that we might be like our parents. For instance, Karen, a wife in our group, has a mother who requires a lot of attention from her children. She wants most family activities to include her. If her grown daughters plan separate activities with their families at holidays, Karen's mother berates them with jealous anger. Karen has so much fear of being like her mother that she has gone to the opposite extreme and will not ask for any special attention for herself. Karen needs to develop her own definition of mothering about which she can feel comfortable—not merely to avoid being like her mother.

Life Experiences

M. Scott Peck, a Christian psychiatrist, tells a mythic story that depicts how a group of people changed their identities and, as a result, their behavior.[8] The story, "The Rabbi's Gift," is about an old, dying monastery that had dwindled to only five monks. The brothers were a critical, miserable, suffering bunch, always complaining. They sought help from the local rabbi. He told them that one of them was the Messiah. They began to treat each other with great care because that is how one would relate to a messiah. Each developed respect for *himself* on the off chance that he might be the Messiah. Visitors noticed the newly tranquil and loving relationships among the brothers. More visitors came to picnic or meditate. They began to recommend the order to their young men, who chose to join. When the monks' identity was that of crotchety old men in a lonely, dying order, they behaved that way with each other. When the rabbi suggested one of them might be the Messiah, they were transformed into monks who behaved like a messiah, and their world responded to the love and peace that was evident in their community. The monastery became a thriving spiritual center as a result of the brothers' change in identity. None of the monks was *really* the Messiah, but the possibility that one *might* be changed their response to life. Similarly, we do not know who we *really* are, but who we believe ourselves to be determines how we act.

Our perception of our identity changes throughout life. It can evolve slowly or change suddenly through an event that causes us to see ourselves differently. As we mature, we develop capabilities by which we express our identity. We develop certain talents and learn to avoid behavior that would shape other talents, depending on what we (or our parents) think is important and meaningful. For example, if you are interested in cooking and you think you could be a chef, you will need to study and/or train with a master chef to develop the necessary capabilities and skills. If you believe you are talented in math and science and would like to be an engineer, there is a path for learning how to fulfill that identity. Likewise, if you want to be a loving husband, or loving parent, you can acquire those capabilities as well. Our perception of our identity determines what we think we are capable of doing. I believe that God made us to benefit ourselves and others, and all parts of us have the potential for being positive. If you think a part of your identity is negative, you can transform that part by going through many of the processes in this course.

My own identity developed, as is the case with most people, in slow stages sometimes, but some experiences created dramatic shifts. My identity changed suddenly at one point from a reluctant to an enthusiastic student. As a young child I was shy and had few friends. I went to my first three grades in progressive, urban schools. I disliked school. I remember being appalled when I learned I would have to attend school for twelve years. But, a cooperative child, I did what was required.

At the end of the third grade we moved to my grandfather's house in the deep woods of Mississippi. I spent the summer catching lizards in the wood pile, chasing blue jays out of the grape vines with slingshots, playing checkers with my grandfather, and reading an occasional comic book. A week before school started, my mother brought home my fourth-grade books. I read all of them that week. When I started school I noticed the work was much easier than I had ever encountered. Two weeks after school started, the principal called me to his office and asked if I would like to go into the fifth grade. These were the days before parents were consulted about such an important decision in a child's life. I agreed I'd like to try the fifth grade and was introduced to the class and teacher.

What took me completely by surprise was that by recess the whole school found out that I had skipped the fourth grade, and I was a hero. I was paraded around the playground and introduced to kids I did not know. I was invited to play games. There was no going back to the fourth grade. In one swift moment my identity changed from reluctant schoolgirl to outstanding student.

Now that my identity had been created, I had to live up to it. My fifth-grade teacher was one of the most difficult in the school. I stayed up late studying. My parents were dubious about the wisdom of this change in my life but supported my efforts. I had narrowed the gap between me and the other fifth-graders by the time we moved to a permanent home and new school. I transferred to the fifth grade in my new school without anyone suspecting I should not have been there. I was, by all rights, a fifth-grader. And I had learned to study. I discovered I enjoyed learning and I liked making good grades.

DISCUSSION 1. *What are some of the physical attributes and talents you inherited? Share some of these with your spouse.*

DISCUSSION 2. *What were some of the names you were called as a child? Did you like them? Who were you to your parents?*

DISCUSSION 3. *What did you learn about your gender from your family? Was there a difference in how boys and girls were treated? How did you feel about the differences? Share these thoughts with your spouse.*

DISCUSSION 4. *Think about an experience that changed your direction in life and your identity. Name that experience in your journal and then share it with your spouse.*

Discerning God's Call

As one Recreating Marriage participant said with enthusiasm, "God calls me to be the best John that I can be." His excitement came from realizing that he did not need to be somebody else to fulfill God's purpose. He could be himself! God does not just call prophets and saints. God calls all of us: simple folk and mental giants, creative people and servants, followers and leaders, the charismatic and the ignored. We feel passion, vitality, and peace of mind when we discern who we are and what our values are and develop capabilities through our lifetime that express those values.

Many people associate the word "call" with a call to ministry or a religious vocation. But it can refer to any vocation. I am broadening the meaning of "call" to refer to being a particular kind of person, to being yourself. In the words of Henry Anderson, pastor emeritus of Fairmount Presbyterian Church, "Life is a called existence."[9] This call encompasses vocation, family roles, health, relaxation, and contribution to community and church.

This broader meaning of "call" can be a relief to some people. Often people think God's call is a heavy-duty responsibility to which they hope they are *not* called. But being called to be your best self can be embraced with enthusiasm. You don't have to be someone who doesn't fit.

Discerning what is most important in your life requires a spiritual journey. Your life is determined by the choices you make. Wiser and more satisfying choices can be made with awareness of your deepest nature and God's grace. Your spiritual journey will be enriched by getting to know yourself better, making more intentional choices about values and beliefs, using a journal for reflection and meditation, and being more receptive to your spouse and other people and thereby encountering God. (A helpful book about preparing for and making the Christian spiritual journey is *Soul Feast*, by Marjorie Thompson, published by Westminster John Knox Press.)

A spiritual journey enriches a marriage and leads to an abundant life filled with passion and vitality. An abundant life is not one filled with things. It is life filled with self-expression that serves other people and God. When you encounter your partner with openness and vulnerability, you find God. Recreating Marriage leads to encounter with yourself, your partner, and God.

DISCUSSION 5. *Think of an important decision you made and write it in your journal. Your decision might have been to take a particular job, to volunteer in a special way, to get married, or to move. You may have had doubts and misgivings at the time of the decision, but you made the choice. What process did you go through? Tell your partner how you knew which choice was right for you.*

When Spouses Do Not Support Each Other

In many marriages, a lack of support between spouses is more common than is clear and generous support. It is important to feel our partner truly values us. We must reveal ourselves in order to feel accepted and intimate. Self-disclosure is a process that can last a lifetime because our identities are growing and developing. Some of you do not feel loved or valued, or you may not love your spouse. I have had enough experience with Recreating Marriage to know that many people feel unloved or unloving. No matter how you feel about yourself or partner now, your feelings may change as you learn new communication skills.

Some spouses support their partners as long as the partner agrees with them, but not when differences occur. Different opinions, values, choices, and feelings do not have to cause disagreements, but often they do because most people do not know how to live with differences. Instead of teaching how to support each other's differences, our culture teaches us three other ways of living with differences: domination, submission, and withdrawal. *Domination* means trying to get your own way by using a variety of means, from persuasion to intimidation. *Submission* means giving up on yourself and doing what others want in order to avoid conflict. *Withdrawal* means doing what you want to without regard for your spouse, and turning off your emotions toward your spouse.

There is, however, a fourth way to deal with difference. It is mutual problem solving, which involves clear and direct communication skills. *Recreating Marriage* teaches you how to do that so that your marriage can be a partnership that supports you and your spouse.

DISCUSSION 6. *Recall a time when you felt really accepted by your spouse. What were you doing? What did you feel? Tell your spouse about that time.*

For Practice

What roles might you enjoy that you have not yet developed? What resources would you need in order to develop this new aspect of your identity?

NOTES

1. Michael E. Kerr and Murray Bowen, *Family Evaluation* (New York: W. W. Norton & Co., 1988).

2. James Hillman, *The Soul's Code: In Search of Character and Calling* (New York: Random House, 1996).

3. Thomas Moore, *Care of the Soul* (New York: HarperCollins, 1992).

4. Thomas Merton, *New Seeds of Contemplation* (New York: New Directions Publishing, 1972).

5. Andrew Weil, *Spontaneous Healing* (New York: Alfred A. Knopf, 1995).

6. Carl Rogers, "A Theory of Therapy, Personality, and Interpersonal Relationships, as Developed in the Client-Centered Framework," in *Psychology: A Study of a Science*, vol. 1: *General Systematic Formulations, Learning, and Special Process*, ed. S. Koch (New York: McGraw-Hill, 1959).

7. Jenny Friedman, "Beyond Pink and Blue," *American Baby* (March 1995).

8. M. Scott Peck, *A Different Drum* (New York: Simon & Schuster, 1989).

9. Henry W. Anderson, "Life Lived with Theological Perspective," *Adult Forum* (Seattle: Plymouth Church, 1995).

Chapter Three

What Are Your Preferences?

When you and your spouse better understand each other, you can talk about your differences with respect. This chapter will help you and your spouse understand and appreciate each other through use of Myers-Briggs preferences.

Identity Contains Preferences

You like to talk and your partner prefers reading a good book. You like to make a budget and stick to it, and your partner prefers a "ballpark estimate" of the checkbook. You like to express your feelings and your partner has a rational solution for everything. You like spontaneous activities and your spouse won't do anything without planning ahead. The person you fell in love with is maddening to live with! To have a happy marriage you must appreciate and encourage each other's personality. In a relationship (and in life) we feel satisfied, fulfilled, and happy when we use our personality to its greatest advantage.

The Myers-Briggs[1] framework provides couples with clear language for appreciating each other's identities, and thus bringing out the best in each other. The Myers-Briggs categories of preferences and temperaments are a way of explaining differences, strengths, and weaknesses in an affirmative way. In the 1920s psychologist Carl Jung wrote about the fundamental "preferences." These preferences relate to the kinds of experiences that people naturally enjoy. People differ in their preferences just as they differ in such features as height, bone density, and skin color.

In the 1950s Katharine Briggs and her daughter, Isabel Myers, using Jung's work as a foundation, developed the Myers-Briggs Type Indicator (MBTI), a tool with which people could measure their preferences and understand themselves. Briggs and Myers revised and categorized Jung's preferences in pairs: (1) Extroversion/Introversion, (2) Sensation/iNtuition, (3) Thinking/Feeling, and (4) Judging/Perceiving. The Myers-Briggs system of understanding people is widely used in education, organization development, and counseling. The categories are often abbreviated by letters: *E, I, S, N* (iNtuition), *T, F, J, P.**

One couple, leaders in our church community, were greatly relieved to learn about their Myers-Briggs types.

Bob is an outgoing, creative ENTP. He loves his work as a factory manager. His wife, Anne, is a quiet, attentive ISFJ. As we got to know her, she revealed she was feeling unloved, in spite of her husband's declaration of his commitment to her. He spent a lot of time playing tennis and other sports after work. He would tell her when he planned to be home and change plans at the last minute. She felt she was doing all the giving—caring for the children, home, and meals, and being available for Bob whenever he was around. When Anne and Bob learned about their personalities, their behavior made sense. Anne could see that Bob's behavior, making last-minute changes and not noticing her needs, did not result from the lack of love for her, but was his natural behavior. Recognizing this, Anne felt more confidence to be a much tougher negotiator. In turn, Bob recognized that he liked the warmth and sensitivity of his Feeling-type wife, and he became less cavalier in his behavior toward her. He realized that commitment to a specific time was much more important to her than to him, and he began to share the details of his plans with her and changed them only when it was really important to do so.

Couples benefit from knowing the Myers-Briggs method of understanding people because it gives them so much appreciation for each other. It frames positively behavior that might be misunderstood. It leads to mutual acceptance because a couple can see how each is similar to many people and different from others. Spouses learn the benefits of each person's particular preference, which enhances good feelings about the self and the spouse. They can also learn that what appear to be weaknesses are strengths that have been exaggerated and can be balanced. A weakness that some spouses notice about their partner, for example, is in planning ahead. People who are not able to plan ahead will miss deadlines and commitments, irritating their family members. However, couples will learn that spouses who are not planners function well in circumstances that call for an immediate response, such as an impromptu performance, spontaneous play, or a crisis. When spontaneous partners are *appreciated* for what they contribute to the relationship, they are more cooperative in learning to plan ahead to keep commitments.

---

* For the remainder of this book, the letter *n* will be capitalized in the words *intuition* and *intuitive* to remind the reader of the personality type indicator that is used for this category.

No Myers-Briggs preference is superior to another. Each has its benefits and weaknesses. However, some preferences are better suited to certain circumstances. For example, Sensing preference is better suited to managing facts of budgeting and the Perceiving preference is better for handling a crisis. To be happy in life and in a marriage it is important to know in which circumstances your set of preferences might flourish so that you can work with your spouse to develop an environment that suits both of you.

Our preferences are a central part of our identity, and have a profound effect on everything we do, including our marriages. They determine whether we are flexible or structured; expressive or restrained; whether we plan budgets, child-care routines, and vacations or are spontaneous in these activities; whether we appreciate celebrations of birthdays, anniversaries, and other relationship markers or think those events are irrelevant. Knowing these behaviors are natural and not personally directed, we can talk about them and solve problems. The behavior is not a statement about a partner's worth.

Preference may seem like an unusual term to describe personality. A more familiar example would be a preference for ice cream. If you go to the freezer routinely, spend your money on ice cream frequently, and often stop by an ice cream stand for a cone, your preference for ice cream organizes your life in a small way. Now suppose you have a preference for Extroversion. This is a preference for an active, people-oriented life. Your Extroversion would organize the activities you enjoy, the kind of work you like, and how you spend your money.

After living with a partner for a while, you can easily describe your partner's habits and quirks. It is better to be able to do more than describe habits. It is useful to know how those habits fit into a pattern so that you can talk about them, recognize why you or your spouse is behaving in such a way, affirm the benefits of that behavior, and balance the inevitable weaknesses. We choose, or prefer, certain life experiences over others. Although people are complex, the four pairs of preferences listed above explain a great deal about behavior, as Craig and Molly learned.

Craig and Molly, married for eight years, own a photography business together. Their relationship was filled with argument when it wasn't frozen in resentment. Molly had great commitment to details. She planned her work days using lists and planned months ahead for larger projects. She delivered customer's orders on time. Molly was anxious and driven much of the time. She hardly ever took time to enjoy herself. Craig was laid-back. He worked from one priority to the next without a lot of planning. Sometimes he was late because he had too much to do at the last minute, but he did not worry about it. Frequently he told Molly he would do something for which he could not find time. Molly had little respect for Craig's management style. To her, he was lazy and ineffective. He, in turn, was depressed about her constant criticism and constant work.

Craig and Molly are different personality types. When they learned about their Myers-Briggs preferences, they discovered that their differences could actually contribute to making a stronger, happier team. They learned that Molly's planning structured the time and resources for their business. Craig's spontaneous, just-in-time approach gave him the flexibility to handle last-minute needs and crises. He learned to respect his own style but also to keep his agreements or renegotiate them. Molly regained respect for Craig and started taking time away from work to relax. These changes happened gradually.

Recognizing Your Preferences

The concepts developed by Myers and Briggs are easily understood. There are four pairs of preferences:

Extroversion	Introversion
Sensation	iNtuition
Thinking	Feeling
Judging	Perceiving

My own description of the four preferences is drawn from my experience and the sources listed in the notes. You can get an idea about what type you may be by looking at the preferences described below and comparing yourself to those descriptions. As you read about the preferences, try to recognize yourself. Mark the one in each pair with which you feel most comfortable and seems most like you. Everyone is a blend of each preference; that is what gives the personality balance and enables us to understand those traits in others. However, everyone has a degree to which she or he feels comfortable with one preference over the other.

You may use one preference at work and another at home. For the purposes of your marriage, it is important to know what preferences you enjoy most, regardless of your requirements at work. Many jobs reward Extroversion (being outgoing), Sensing (attention to detail), Thinking (logical decision making), and Judging (planning and order).

You may have taught yourself certain behaviors in order to do some jobs successfully, although the preferences may not be natural for you. But you will be most happy in your intimate relationship if you can be yourself. Compare each preference to what you most enjoy at home.

Ask your spouse to give his or her impressions of your preferences and compare those with how you see yourself. What seems most attractive may not necessarily be you. If you decide you are one type and your spouse thinks you behave as a different type, you may not have a strong preference in a particular area, or you may be understanding the preferences differently. Continue exchanging information with each other until you achieve clarity. The purpose of the exercise is to gain greater understanding, not to argue about who is right. Don't get discouraged when you notice differences. You will learn later how to deal with them.

Extroversion—Introversion Preferences

These preferences are related to *where* you focus attention and derive the most pleasure: either the external world or your internal experience. Extroverts, as you might guess, focus externally. Introverts focus internally.

People Who Are Extroverts (E)	People Who Are Introverts (I)
Feel energized and excited about being with people. They generally don't mind being with new people or groups of people.	Prefer one-to-one contact or people they know very well. Being around new people or large groups drains them of energy.
Feel uncomfortable with much time alone.	Feel refreshed and energized after time alone; in fact, require time alone to gather their thoughts.
Talk without thinking an idea through completely.	Rehearse conversation internally before speaking. They practice the adage, "Think before you act."
Stand out as speakers in conversations; have more difficulty being listeners.	Are better listeners in a conversation and may have difficulty getting points across unless they have thought through a presentation.
Prefer working in a team to getting things done alone.	Prefer working alone or with one other person to working with a group.

People Who Are Extroverts (E)	People Who Are Introverts (I)
Prefer a large "playing field" without specifying boundaries.	Prefer a "playing field" that is small enough for them to control directly. They are more protective of their own territory and less likely to intrude into other people's territories.
May be accused by their spouses of intruding into other people's territories, taking or controlling what does not belong to them.	May be accused by their spouses of selfishness or inhibition, not sharing their things, time, or thoughts.
May be appreciated by their spouses for being expressive and providing comfort to friends and relatives.	May be appreciated by their spouses for having the ability to listen, and their thorough and thoughtful responses.

Nate is an extrovert. He is well known in our neighborhood. Extroverted Jon knows all the kids on the street and has visited their houses frequently. Extroverted Ariana has many friends from school and theater activities. We hardly see her except by arrangement. I am an Introvert. I know two families well and know little about the others except what Nate and Jon tell me. On the other hand, the family members come to talk to me because they know that I am a good listener.

DISCUSSION 1. *Discuss with your spouse the list of Extroversion— Introversion preferences. Which list fits you best? Do you have a strong preference or a mild preference for one over the other?*

DISCUSSION 2. *How have your Extroversion or Introversion preferences affected your life together? Describe an event in which you could clearly recognize your spouse's preference.*

Sensing—iNtuition Preferences

These preferences identify *which kind* of stimulation you enjoy and on which your attention naturally focuses. This preference pair is a bit more subtle, but is significant in creating harmony or conflict among people. Simply put, the Sensing preference is for specific and real information, while iNtuitive preference is for general and imaginative information.

People Who Prefer Sensing (S)	People Who Prefer iNtuition (N)
Prefer stimulation through the five senses—seeing, hearing, touching, tasting, and smelling. Sensory experiences represent facts and "reality."	Prefer stimulation from mental processes, such as analyzing ideas or abstract concepts.
Deal with what is present and tangible in life. Prefer action to thinking. Thinking is boring. Are the *builders and maintainers* of society.	Prefer thinking about possibilities. Like to compare what they already have to an ideal they have created in their minds. Action is a repetition of something they have thought, and therefore boring. Are the *creators* of society.
Like working with specifics and details such as facts and figures, recipes, checkbooks, lawnmowers, computers, and other items they can get their hands on. Impatient with theories.	Like working with general ideas such as why some people are more romantic or how the schools could be improved. Impatient with details of applying the ideas.
Work hands-on to solve problems in the practical, real world rather than thinking about how the problem fits into the big picture.	Like to solve problems in the world of ideas or fantasy first, and may or may not apply their solutions to the real world.
Enjoy conversation about what they did with people and things during their day as well as the joys and problems encountered.	Enjoy conversation about ideas, thoughts, and feelings they have had, and especially what they could do in the future.
Creativity is by experimentation, trial, and error. Become expert at repeated actions such as sports, cooking, physical care of people, or home maintenance.	Creativity is done by thinking something through first, then trying it. Prefer to design a creative project and have someone else do it, such as planning a vacation and having the spouse get the tickets, arrange for child care, and pack.
Want others to tell them clear expectations and guidelines.	Want to know overall results and figure out the expectations and guidelines for themselves.
May be accused by their spouses of being a nitpicker about details.	May be accused by their spouses of not communicating clearly and being unrealistic.

People Who Prefer Sensing (S)	People Who Prefer iNtuition (N)
May be appreciated by their spouses for giving attention to checkbooks, food, laundry, cars, lawn, household maintenance, insurance policies, doctor's appointments, kids' schedules, and all the processes of daily life.	May be appreciated by their spouses for having the ability to create interesting, dynamic projects and activities as well as solving complex problems.

Nate and I are both iNtuitive, but Nate much more so than I. He loves to talk about his philosophies. For him, everything is possible, from sailing around the world to owning his own company. Never mind that we don't have an ocean-going sailboat or know how to navigate. Or that we don't have millions to buy a company. These are minor obstacles to be overcome. I, too, am iNtuitive, but much stronger in Sensing than Nate and thus more reality-oriented. I am excited by Nate's ideas, and am iNtuitive enough to understand them. I often work out the problems so we can accomplish Nate's visions, such as educating us about navigation, weather, and sailing skills. Ariana is iNtuitive and can join in with Nate in lively conversations, although she laughs at his philosophizing sometimes. Jon is Sensing, and often gets left out of these conversations. Being Extroverted, he hardly notices, and creates a conversation of his own, describing in endless detail the fish in his aquarium, the latest "Simpsons" episode, or his hockey game. It has been very important to understand Jon's Sensing nature, because Nate and I are prone to give general instructions for chores and family rules. Jon does not respond to generalities, and even makes a game of not getting the message. We have learned to be *very* specific with him.

When one spouse is Sensing and the other is iNtuitive, they can feel like they are using two different languages. Sensing and iNtuitive types tend to be critical of the other, but if they can appreciate the gifts the other brings they can be a marvelous team.

DISCUSSION 3. *Discuss with your spouse which list of Sensing—iNtuition preferences fits you best. Do you have a strong preference or a mild preference for one over the other?*

DISCUSSION 4. *How have your preferences for Sensing or iNtuition affected your marriage? Describe an event when you could clearly recognize the preference of your spouse.*

Thinking—Feeling Preferences

These preferences are related to how or by what process we make decisions. A person with the Thinking preference makes more logical, objective decisions, whereas the one with the Feeling preference makes emotion-based, people-oriented decisions. For example, a logical, Thinking person will approach a decision with, "Will this work?" Whereas an emotional, Feeling person might ask, "How will this affect us?" The stereotypical masculine approach is Thinking. Sixty percent of American males are this type. The stereotypical feminine decision is Feeling, maybe because 65 percent of American women are Feeling.[2] Remember that some men and women do not follow the stereotype.

People Who Prefer Thinking (T)	People Who Prefer Feeling (F)
Are rational decision makers, relying on logical methods to reach conclusions.	Are emotional decision makers, relying on empathy with people to reach conclusions.
Focus on fairness within the family. Tend to want rules and are willing to create them. Have great concern that the family function well and things get done properly.	Focus on the personal experience of people within a situation. Have great concern about the feelings of family members.
Are motivated by long-range results and can endure immediate discomfort to get desired results. The results are what are most important. Are good at disciplining themselves and others.	Are motivated to seek harmony and pleasure inside themselves and with other people. Are reluctant to induce pain. The process is most important. Are good at supporting family members, and affirmation from others is important. Can be easily hurt by distance or momentary rejection.
Are more willing to tell what they are thinking even if it hurts or offends. Are critical of others and silently critical of themselves. Can be easily offended by criticism.	Are more likely to be diplomatic in telling the truth, even if the truth gets distorted in order to protect feelings in themselves and others. May say something nice even if they don't believe it.
Approach love in a practical manner. They feel love when a relationship is fair and productive. They are excited by accomplishing something together. Are angered by systems in the relationship breaking down, promises not kept, things not getting done effectively.	Experience love by a projection of an ideal image of the person. Feel love when the relationship is harmonious. Like symbols of love such as presents, notes, and unexpected phone calls. Expect the best in people. Are hurt by broken contact or emotional distance in a relationship.

People Who Prefer Thinking (T)	People Who Prefer Feeling (F)
May be accused by their spouses of being uncaring and unexpressive. Their love may be hidden behind concern for good behavior. They may discipline children too much. Children may feel demands without support.	May be accused by their spouses of being driven by their feelings without getting results. They may not discipline children enough. Children may not get clear messages about what is expected.
May be appreciated by their spouses for being fair and having a rational ability to solve problems. Children may feel pride in what they can accomplish with hard work if there is adequate reward for performance.	May be appreciated by their spouses for being warm, empathetic, and giving attention to the family's emotional life. Children feel loved and wanted if there is adequate discipline.

Nate and I differ from the usual male-female pattern in that I am the Thinking type and he is the Feeling one. That keeps things interesting. Nate enjoys making the family feel good by doing little favors for us. He frequently makes meals (the iNtuitive way, *not* by using a recipe!). He is not big on family rules but prefers to live by what seems most important at the moment. He is full of affirmation for everyone, just for being who they are. He is sensitive to my disapproval, and calls me a "barracuda" when he thinks I am being coldly determined. Typical of a Thinking/Feeling couple, we had conflicts in the area of disciplining the children. Nate preferred explaining things and encouraging the children. I thought he was ineffective in changing Jon's behavior. I preferred rewards and consequences. He thought I was heartless. After many conversations over about two years, we worked out a good system of balance in which the kids feel loved and understood as well as disciplined.

Do you recognize these people? They—or others with similar traits—are part of your life.

DISCUSSION 5. *Discuss with your spouse each person's preference for decision making. Does the Thinking or the Feeling list fit you best? How do your preferences affect your relationship? Do you have a strong preference or a mild preference for one or the other?*

DISCUSSION 6. *How have your preferences for Feeling or Thinking affected your marriage? Describe an event when you could clearly recognize your spouse's preference.*

Judging—Perceiving Preferences

These preferences refer to how you *organize* your time, space, and thinking. Judging types naturally categorize things, people, time, and ideas. Perceiving types enjoy the flow of experiences without necessarily categorizing them. This is more easily understood when you read the following descriptions.

People Who Prefer Judging (J)	People Who Prefer Perceiving (P)
Enjoy putting things in categories. Things in the house have a place. Certain behavior has a proper time and place. Decisions are easy when the categories are known.	Enjoy simply receiving stimulation or information. Do not necessarily categorize and do not have particular places for things or proper time for activities. Decisions are made only when circumstances require them.
Organize time in a segmented schedule to accomplish a goal. Become uncomfortable when life is too spontaneous.	Experience life as a flow of events rather than a segmented schedule. Like to experience where life takes them rather than control where life takes them by setting goals. Become uncomfortable when life is too scheduled.
Are most comfortable planning ahead. Plan to avoid crisis and get upset when a crises occurs.	Are most comfortable with spontaneous, unplanned activities. Are effective in a crisis and enjoy the challenge.
Like to complete projects to feel accomplished. May procrastinate when they fear failure.	Enjoy the process of a project. Completion is not necessary to feel accomplished. May procrastinate doing unpleasant tasks.
May be accused by their spouses of being rigid, not enough fun, and judgmental. Men of this type may depend on their wives to create an orderly home environment, whether or not their wife is of the same type.	May be accused by their spouses of being disorganized, indecisive, and not goal-oriented.
May be appreciated by their spouses for being dependable, having an orderly environment, and planning for the future.	May be appreciated by their spouses for being relaxed and easy-going, having a playful manner on a daily basis, and having the ability to respond well in a crisis.

Nate and Jon are Perceiving types and Ariana and I are Judging. It has required a lot of genuine understanding and working together to make this combination successful. When Judging/Perceiving differences are strong in family members, they interfere with the daily lives of the others. The Judging person feels intruded upon by spontaneous activity that feels out of control, such as in the area of financial management, family activities, and home care. For Perceiving persons, organization is not a natural act, and they experience a request for organization as an unreasonable demand. Nate is typical of the Perceiving type in that he does not think about organizing as he goes along. When we first met, I noticed he put anything anywhere. Granted, kitchen equipment was relegated in the general direction of the kitchen, papers were maintained in one office room, and Jon's things were everywhere. He thinks his organization was much more refined than that. We agree to disagree and it does not matter, because when we got married, I created places for things to go and Nate happily cooperated. Jon cooperated not so happily, but over the years he has become accustomed to these changes. Ariana felt invaded by clutter when Nate and Jon joined our family, and she stayed in her room a lot. Eventually a more orderly system was imposed, and she has taken ownership of the whole house in the past few years and invites her friends over to make meals and have parties.

I value Nate's ability to be interrupted at any time to take care of anything. He transports kids around endlessly. He meets with workmen. He welcomes friends for meals, ready or not. He also responds to clients' ongoing needs without much planning. It is stressful for me to have a kid's friend over for a meal or sleepover without planning, but I am better than Nate at producing a complex event such as a party or vacation, which requires planning.

Perceiver Jon never gets school projects done in advance, but has excellent concentration for the last minute. Activities with friends are nearly always spontaneous. His favorite activity is growing things: vegetables in his garden and fish in his aquariums. He continually exchanges one fish for another, and changes the rock gardens and ceramic doodads in the tank. One thing flows into another without apparent completion.

DISCUSSION 7. *With your spouse's assistance, decide whether you are a Judging or Perceiving type. Sometimes spouses are Judging in one arena and Perceiving in another. For example, a man may be completely passive about household activities because he does not recognize that as his territory, appearing to be a Perceiving type. But at work he may be highly organized, more Judging.*

If this is your situation, ask yourself in which lifestyle you are happier. Knowing what makes you happy will help you become more intentional in creating the lifestyle you want.

DISCUSSION 8. *Discuss how your types have affected your marriage. Describe an event when you could clearly recognize your spouse's preference.*

Putting Yourself Together

You have selected four preferences. You should have four letters, representing your four preferences. For example, I am an INTJ; Nate, an ENFP; Ariana, an ENTJ; and Jon, an ESTP. As you become familiar with these preferences, you may recognize others' types, such as those of your parents and children, and you can then try to communicate to that kind of person in their style rather than communicating in your own style all the time and miscommunicating. You may discover that you have been irritated when communicating with persons with preferences different from your own because you don't naturally understand each other. Understanding people by preference creates respect. Myers-Briggs typing affirms differences instead of labeling them in a negative way. As one of my clients in marriage counseling said, "My wife says I'm flaky. Now I know I'm just iNtuitive!"

Once you understand your preferences and your spouse's, you can try to work together to create the kind of life you want. Trying to *change* your partner's type will create a lot of frustration for both of you. However, you and your partner can learn to use your strengths and balance your weaknesses. For example, Brian, an adventurous ENTP, was unhappy in his marriage because he saw Cindy, his ISFJ wife, as inadequate. In his mind, she was rigid and fearful of new activities. He wanted a companion who could enjoy scuba diving, traveling, and athletic activities. She was content to take care of their three young children, decorate their home impeccably, cook wonderful meals, and maintain close relations with their extended family. After Brian learned about their personality types, he could see that his wife was perfectly normal and made an important contribution to their marriage. He stopped trying to change her. They had problems to solve, such as how he could enjoy some of his activities and develop friends with similar interests. His wife encouraged him to take a few vacations alone, which made him appreciate her even more.

Children's Preferences Can Affect a Marriage

As you learn about your marriage, you will naturally be reminded of your parents' relationship and how they were parents to you. You will also notice your children and how their personalities affect you. Some preferences of children are noticeable when they are very young. Extroversion and Introversion are easy to identify early. Children with Feeling preference are very sensitive to praise and conflict. Children who are iNtuitive get carried away by their fantasy world.

Different ideas about parenting are one of the most common sources of discord in marriages. Not only must parents contend with their own differences when parenting, but they have to cope with the different personalities of their children. If you and your child share preferences, you will probably understand and empathize with him or her much more than if your child were different from you. You will automatically know what kind of parenting would benefit your child, because you know what you wanted when you were young. But your spouse may not understand.

Allison and Ray have two very different children, who actually reflect their own differences. Their son is sensitive, affectionate, and cooperative, probably possessing Introvert and Feeling preferences similar to his mother. Their daughter is outgoing, competitive, and argumentative, possibly with Extroversion and Thinking among her preferences like her father. Ray delights in his daughter as he encourages her accomplishments. He is proud of her outspokenness, but he is a little embarrassed that his son is not more aggressive, particularly in athletics. Allison gets exasperated by what seems unmannerly and annoying in their daughter, much preferring the company of their sweet-tempered son. These parents can easily form mother/son and father/daughter alliances where the pairs are more caring with each other than with other family members.

You will naturally be sympathetic to a child similar to yourself, an enjoyable feeling that is not to be avoided. However, it is crucial to the well-being of your family that you develop good communication skills so that you are able to maintain a healthy, nurturing relationship with each of your children, even those most different from you.

From my work counseling parents, I have come to appreciate how strongly children are influenced by their inherited preferences. You must try to bring out the best in the personality your child was born with, but you do not create the child's natural tendencies. You can encourage what is there, helping a child develop a positive identity, or you can discourage a child's nature and contribute to depression and frustration in a child. An energetic, curious, extroverted child can completely exhaust two quiet, introverted parents unless they learn how to provide lots of opportunity for running, screaming, climbing, and playing with other children. Conversely, I have seen two extroverted parents wonder where they went wrong because their child preferred to spend long hours with books and music.

DISCUSSION 9. *Discuss whether each of your children is an Introvert or Extrovert. What experiences will each child need for pleasure and enrichment?*

DISCUSSION 10. *How does your children's introversion or extroversion affect your life and marriage?*

DISCUSSION 11. *Identify whether each of your parents is an Introvert or an Extrovert. How did your parents' preferences affect you as you were growing up?*

Learning about Myers-Briggs preferences will help you understand that there are many ways to be healthy and normal. As you learn to value all aspects of personality, you will grow in appreciation of yourself, your spouse, and your children, even though they may be different from you. You will be more intentional about finding activities that satisfy you and each member of your family.

In the next chapter, you will learn about temperaments, which are based on a combination of two preferences. Temperaments make behavior patterns seem more distinct and recognizable than do preferences. If you have had any problem selecting your preferences and think perhaps that you are right in the middle of one pair, learning about temperaments may help you decide what you are.

For Practice

Discuss a project you have accomplished as a couple, perhaps a vacation. How did each person's preferences contribute to that project?

NOTES

1. David Keirsey and Marilyn Bates, *Please Understand Me* (Del Mar, Calif.: Prometheus Nemesis Book Co., 1984); Isabel Briggs Myers, *Gifts Differing* (Palo Alto, Calif.: Consulting Psychologists Press, 1983); and Otto Kroeger and Janet Thresen, *Type Talk* (New York: Delacorte Press).

2. Isabel Briggs Myers and Mary H. McCaulley, *Manual: A Guide to the Development and Use of the Myers-Briggs Type Indicator* (Palo Alto, Calif.: Consulting Psychologists Press, 1985).

Chapter Four

What Are Your Temperaments?

In this chapter you will identify your temperament, which is a combination of two preferences. You will learn about your strengths and your spouse's as you learn about temperaments. You may better accept your spouse's weaknesses as well as your own, as you learn that weaknesses are actually strengths that are carried too far.

The Four Temperaments

Temperaments have been described by observers of human behavior since Hippocrates, but the Myers-Briggs description of temperaments is particularly useful in describing couple interaction. Temperaments provide more richness and depth of personality than do the four preferences separately. They provide information you need to understand yourself and your partner without overloading you with details.

The way your preferences are combined makes a great difference in what you enjoy and how you act. When you learned your preferences, you identified yourself in four categories and concluded with four initials, such as INTJ. Each preference combines with the other three to produce a particular pattern of behavior. For example, when a person has Sensing combined with Judging, the Sensing preference for the tangible and factual part of life adds to the Judging preference for predictability and organization. This person loves to organize a home, an office, a hospital, or anything in that person's life. All the details of his or her life are planned. If a person's Sensing preference is combined with Perceiving, you have a person who still enjoys the tangible and factual part of life, but instead of being predictable and organized, the person enjoys spontaneous and unstructured activity, such as impromptu entertaining and crisis intervention. The home of this kind of person might be topsy-turvy, and action and fun are more important than order.

Then add either Introversion or Extroversion. An Introverted, Sensing, Judging type would be an organized person who likes a limited number of people and activities, but becomes technically expert in whatever activity they choose. This person's home would be quiet, peaceful, and well-maintained. But an Extroverted, Sensing, Judging type would be an organized person who likes a lot of activity and relationships with many people. This person's home would be buzzing with people on various schedules. Life for this person would be loaded with activities but still highly organized and well-maintained.

Now, add to this mix a preference for Feeling or Thinking. For example, an ESJ person with Feeling preference would be an organized person who likes a lot of activity and relationships with many people, and that activity would be directed toward caring for people. Examples of these activities are teaching or caring for children or sick people. On the other hand, an ESJ person with a Thinking preference would be an organized person who likes a lot of activity and relationships with many people, and that activity might be directed toward managing things such as organizing a factory or a business. There are possibilities of an ESTJ or ISTJ; an ESTP or ISTP; an ESFJ or ISFJ; an ESFP or ISFP. And there are the same number of combinations for the iNtuitives, making a total of sixteen possible combinations of type. Whew! You would not want to remember the descriptions of each of type. Narrowing the combinations to four temperaments makes it much easier to comprehend.

By combining two preferences of your four initials, we can simplify these sixteen personality types into four general categories of personalities, called temperaments. You have only four categories to remember, rather than sixteen possible combinations of preferences. The four temperaments are as follows:

> Sensing combined with Judging (SJ)
> Sensing combined with Perceiving (SP)
> iNtuition combined with Feeling (NF)
> iNtuition combined with Thinking (NT)

You may wonder why the Sensing preference is combined with J or P, whereas the iNtuitive preference is combined with F or T, to create a temperament. I use the the temperament combinations described by Keirsey and Bates[1] for Recreating Marriage because I find they are more dynamic and meaningful for couples. Actually some authors, Isabel Myers in *Gifts Differing,*[2] for example, combine Sensing with T or F and iNtuition with T or F.

What Is Your Temperament?

In chapter 2 we focused on the pairs of preferences in the MBTI framework. Those pairs were the following:

Extroversion	Introversion
Sensation	iNtuition
Thinking	Feeling
Judging	Perceiving

You selected one of each pair, giving you four preferences, your four initials (for example, ENTP). To determine your temperament: (1) Write down the four preference initials you identified in chapter 2. For example, I am an INTJ. Look at the four temperaments: SJ, SP, NF, and NT. (2) Determine which temperament is contained in your initials. My temperament is found in my middle initials, NT.

As you read about the four temperaments, see if the temperament corresponding to your preferences is a description of you. It should be, but often, after understanding the temperaments, a person has a better perspective about the preferences themselves. And you may change your choice of preference as a result of learning your temperament. If you were not sure which one of the preferences fit you, you can clarify your preference by noticing which of the temperaments suits you best. For example, you may have been undecided between Feeling or Thinking. Your Myers-Briggs type might have been INFJ or INTJ. You will learn that two of the temperaments are NF and NT. These are quite different patterns of behavior. If you recognize yourself in the NF description, then you have a Feeling preference. Similarly, if you see yourself among the NTs, then you have a preference for Thinking.

If you engage in activities that are necessary but do not suit you, this could confuse your recognition of your temperament. For example, I do a lot of Sensing activities, such as making grocery lists and menus, keeping the family financial records, and organizing Nate's files. I could have chosen ISTJ or INTJ for my Myers-Briggs preferences. However, when I read the two lists of temperaments, I saw that I am clearly an NT rather than an SJ. I enjoy creating systems with logic and order in them, but I actually do not like maintaining the system as an SJ might. I enjoyed helping to set up Nate's filing system, but I would *hate* to file on a weekly basis. Anne, my SJ secretary, seems to really enjoy it.

Of course, when you are strong in a particular temperament, you also have the weaknesses of that temperament. A strength becomes a weakness when there is too much of it. Recognize the temperament as a strength and learn to balance it. For example, if a person is too persnickety about having a few things out of place, affirm the benefits of an orderly household, and discuss how some flexibility can be introduced into the order. It is natural for a partner of one type to criticize a spouse of another type, and a criticized person defends the benefits of what comes naturally to him or her. A conversation acknowledging the strengths of both persons and discussing how to deal with differences is much more effective than criticism. (How to handle strengths that become weaknesses is addressed in the next chapter under "Appreciating Your Spouse's Strengths.")

Most people recognize their type easily after reading the lists of typical traits and discussing them with their partners. However, some people think that two lists apply to them. The lists that most frequently invite confusion are NF and NT. Some people are right in the middle between F and T, so parts of both lists apply. However, people in the middle usually respond in certain circumstances consistently as one or the other. For example, a woman may be an NF with friends, but become critical and demanding with her husband, typical of an NT whose strengths are carried too far. For the purpose of Recreating Marriage, decide how you behave most often in your family, with your spouse and children. In the case above, the woman would be an NT.

Keep in mind that Extroverted types will much more outwardly portray the behavior than the Introverts. The Introverts' behavior may be more subtle.

The SJ Temperament

An SJ personality type combines a realistic, hands-on, detail-oriented person, a Sensing type, with a planned and organized person, a Judging type. SJ types like to take care of people, organizations, and environments in a physical sense. With their Sensing preference they enjoy details and facts, and with their Judging preference they are orderly and decisive. They like to belong to a family with a strong tradition. They like well-established, clearly defined routines and specific roles. Receiving approval is particularly important to this temperament. In marriage they like to keep the mechanisms of life going: children bathed, groceries in stock, and meals made; house repaired, nicely decorated, neat, and clean. They make up about 38 percent of the population.[3]

At their best, SJs:

1. Create an *orderly* household with routines for taking care of people and things. They enjoy handling the details.

2. Are *modest* about their accomplishments, but like others to recognize their achievements.

3. Feel *respect is a strong value.* They behave respectfully toward elders and expect young people to behave respectfully toward them.

4. Enjoy *traditional* roles because traditions let them know clearly what is expected of them and what can be expected in the future.

5. Are comfortable *making decisions*.

6. Handle money by *budgeting*, keeping records, and balancing books.

7. Choose *careers* in administration, teaching children, homemaking, crafts, medical service, and other technical careers.

8. Support their partners by providing an *orderly environment and routine family life*. Spouses may appreciate the SJ's partnership in decision making. The SJ partner can free up a spouse to participate in a career or other creative endeavor by managing family matters.

When SJs carry their strengths too far, they:

1. Create a *rigid* household with routines that do not have meaning for other people and restrict the self-expression of the family.

2. Are *self-effacing* and afraid to take risks.

3. Depend too much on *authoritarian roles* that may take the form of demanding respect not equal to their accomplishments or giving up their own decision making to follow an authority.

4. Become *slaves to traditions* rather than being able to select those traditions most enjoyable to them and the family. May make snap decisions based on history and tradition. Resist change of any kind.

5. Can be *so concerned about the budget* and balanced books that they forget that money is to serve them and not vice versa.

6. Can be so *focused on details* that they miss the bigger picture of what is important to the family. Life may be too serious to be fun. Family may get the material needs met without emotional or spiritual needs cared for.

DISCUSSION 1. *Are you or is your spouse an SJ? Discuss with your spouse whether the lists describe some important aspects of your personality. If you do not recognize either you or your spouse, does the list describe one of your children or parents?*

DISCUSSION 2. *What is it like to live with an SJ spouse? How does SJ behavior affect the family? What special contributions are made to your family by the SJ partner?*

I cannot give you an SJ example from our family because our family of five does not have an SJ member. You would notice that when you come in the door and see the mail all over the dining room, magazines scattered over the living room, a very creative but sloppy aquarium in the corner of the living room, and no plans for dinner. You might think to yourself, "Boy, could this house use an SJ around here!"

I can tell you about my SJ mother, to whom I felt quite inferior until I learned about Myers-Briggs personality types. She got up every morning before anyone else to organize and prepare dinner before she went to work. She prepared breakfast for the family and we all ate together. By 8:30 she was at her full-time job as an office manager and bookkeeper for a school system. After work, she often dropped by the grocery store to pick up whatever was missing. Upon returning home, she finished cooking dinner, served dinner, and cleaned the kitchen—before freezing or canning produce from our productive Mississippi garden. You might wonder what I was doing during this time. Delegating was not one of her strong points.

The SP Temperament

Imagine a person who has the physical presence and love of detail of a Sensing type, and the curiosity of a Perceiving type, and you have an SP. Persons with the SP temperament live life in the excitement of the moment. This type constitutes about 38 percent of the population. Their pleasure is fun-loving, uninhibited action, spontaneity, excitement, and contest. Many love using tools, sports equipment, and instruments. They are great practical problem solvers in a crisis. They have the greatest endurance of all the types for something that captures their attention, but they are often restless, jittery, and bored with activities that don't interest them. They can take on huge projects such as moving residences, redecorating or renovating a house, or throwing a spontaneous party. They add fun to a marriage and family by their entertaining style. SP children, particularly the Extroverted ones, can be mislabeled "hyperactive" by adults who do not understand them. The Introverted SPs can seem inattentive. This type is the least represented in institutions of higher learning. Although SPs may have high intelligence, most educational systems do not reward their natural style of learning by doing.

At their best, SPs:

1. Enjoy practical tasks, as does an SJ, but they bring to those tasks a *playful spirit*. They are great at creating games out of any experience.

2. Are governed by what is immediate and present and are therefore excellent *problem solvers* in a crisis. All projects get done when necessary instead of by prior planning.

3. Are *very flexible* in applying new behavior to problems, including negotiation with creative solutions.

4. Love the *sensuous and pleasurable* aspects of life, and enhance the lives of those around by their enjoyable activities. They are usually gentle and amiable. History and tradition are not relevant unless enjoyable in the present.

5. Enjoy *physical activities* and can acquire great physical skill because of the enjoyment. Are good at sports and crisis intervention such as police, fire fighting, and rescue work. Like to use the machinery, tools, and instruments of laboratories, music, and art, and as a result can become master craftsmen, technicians, musicians, and artists.

6. Enjoy *spending money* for present needs or wants and do not worry about it.

7. Are appreciated for their *wit, light-heartedness, entertainment, flexible cooperation, and ability to handle emergencies*. They easily engage in play with children, and the bonds with children are usually strong.

When SPs carry their strengths too far, they:

1. Can use their playfulness to *distract from serious matters*. Unpleasant conversations or unenjoyable activities can be avoided indefinitely.

2. *Do not plan ahead* enough to avoid a crisis.

3. Are so committed to doing exactly what they want at the moment that they *do not commit to any responsibilities*.

4. May be so oriented to immediate pleasure that family *traditions do not get established*, depriving the more tradition-minded members of security and continuity.

5. Are so physically oriented they *may avoid activities requiring reflection or intellectual work*. They may lack perspective.

6. May *spend beyond their means* and perceive their spouses to be inhibiting their spending. Their disdain for budgets and financial planning may create an unpredictable and insecure future.

7. May seem *like another child* instead of a partner. May not discipline children consistently. In fact, discipline may be missing altogether.

DISCUSSION 3. *Are you or is your spouse an SP? Discuss with your spouse whether the lists describe some important aspects of your personality. If neither of you is an SP, do you recognize a parent or child in the description?*

DISCUSSION 4. *What is it like to live with an SP spouse? How does SP behavior affect the family? What special contributions are made to your family by the SP partner?*

SPs are gentle, kind, and flexible. They generally do not know how to assert themselves with a critical spouse. They prefer to avoid conflict, so conflicts build to a crisis before an SP seeks help.

Our culture does not appreciate or have a place for SPs as children. School environments are often run by SJ teachers who may not have enough appreciation for the physical needs and the concrete, hands-on learning style of SP children. They may grow up feeling like academic failures, hating an academic environment. If they develop some ability to communicate as adults, they are more appreciated for their entertaining nature, courage for taking physical risks, and their artistic abilities.

The SP I know best is my son Jon, who is the Extroverted representation of this type. He is passionate about his interests, and trying to contain his energy in a civilized household is like trying to teach a wild horse to dance. When he is in a new situation he gets so distracted that he misbehaves and therefore upsets the adults around him. This happens at the beginning of new classes at school. His progress reports show he has been irritating his teachers and is just getting by at mid-semester. We assign consequences for his misbehavior and goals to work toward, and by the end of the semester he has pulled up his grades to B and above. Lecturing to him is a waste of words. He learns from behavior. When classroom practice and experiments are provided, Jon shines. He was great in biology, and his teacher took special interest in him. He has four aquariums, one in the living room that is about four feet long, and three smaller ones in his bedroom. He wants to make a new ten-foot aquarium in the basement. He makes frequent trips to the pet store to buy or exchange fish, food, and gadgets for filtering the water. He digs for worms daily. He seems to have no goal about how he wants his aquarium to be when complete. The endless process of creating it seems to be enjoyable. His aspiration is to study fish and wildlife at a college where exploring wilderness is part of the curriculum.

Most SP adults have learned not to be intrusive to other people and to adapt to their surroundings, but it is crucial that they find activities that use their interests. Otherwise, they will be frustrated and depressed. For example, a client consulted me about his memory problem at work. He was very self-critical about his failure to live up to his boss's expectations for record keeping. He recognized that he was an ESFP, someone who enjoys spur-of-the-moment activities with people. He was a good technician and took a lot of pride in his ability to help other people solve their computer problems with little time delay. However, he hated to sit down and focus long enough to write all the details of reporting his daily activities. He had no memory problem at all. He was avoiding what he disliked! Because he was so valued at providing service, he and his boss worked out a system that required less paperwork.

When introverted SPs are distracted by people and events happening near them, they will be less obvious about it than extroverted SPs, but they will be distracted internally. Like extroverted SPs, they need hands-on activities that allow exploration and playfulness so that they can lead productive and enjoyable lives.

The NF Temperament

When you combine the imagination of the iNtuitive with the love of people and harmony of the Feeling type, you have an NF. Persons of the NF temperament, about 12 percent of the population, are idealists about people and relationships. Their iNtuition contributes dreams and fantasies, and their Feeling nature creates an intense interest in people. They can be charismatic, empathetic, and dramatic. They thrive on recognition, caring, and personal attention, particularly to their emotions. They develop a mental model of how the world should be. Much of their conversation, work, and life activities center on how to get their real world to be like the relationships they have created in their minds. They are usually talented communicators. In marriages they contribute warmth, concern for other people's feelings, and emotional affirmation of the family. NFs can be easily hurt by what they perceive as rejection or neglect. Although they usually want to please, they can feel hate toward those who hurt them. Self-improvement is important to them. They think in global and impressionistic terms, and may be difficult for more detail-oriented types to understand.

At their best, NFs:

1. *Understand the emotional needs* of family members and communicate to meet those emotional needs. They are warm and express their love. They see the best in everyone.

2. Have a *lively fantasy life* that can be translated into noble visions for family or community activities, or into stories to entertain family members or to be written for publication.

3. Are *passionate about learning about people*. They may be quiet observers bringing information to promote personal growth in the

family. Their passion may take them to advanced degrees in the humanities or religion.

4. Are motivated most by *finding personal meaning* for their lives. They support their family in developing lives with personal significance and develop careers that help other people find meaning, such as counseling and ministry.

5. Are *very good communicators*, particularly if the communications are positive. They assist other family members in saying what they mean and improving their communication skills. They may find careers in politics or journalism.

6. Often live *very creative lives*. They are led into fields of entertainment and artistic expression by their lively fantasy lives.

7. Are appreciated by their spouses for their *romantic expressions, their encouragement, their sensitive understanding of personal issues, and their promotion of intimacy.*

When NFs carry their strengths too far, they:

1. Are so sensitive to the emotional needs of their family that they can become *overprotective and overly attached*. They may avoid seeing the negative traits in others that need confrontation or discipline. When they finally get around to recognizing flaws in family members their idealized fantasy about the person collapses and they may feel utterly hopeless, betrayed, rejecting, and hateful. The saying, "You never hate someone more than the one you used to love," applies to disappointed NFs.

2. Develop *idealized fantasies*. This gap between their ideal and reality may create intense disappointment, which can be expressed as creatively and vociferously as previous romantic expressions were.

3. May be so passionate in experiencing the varieties of human contact, such as relationships with friends or coworkers, the novel they are writing, or a daring adventure, that they *spread themselves too thin*, leaving their family feeling neglected.

4. Become *very depressed* if unable to discover what is meaningful in their lives. Life can be an unfulfilling search for an unrealized ideal, such as Don Quixote tilting at windmills.

5. May *communicate so much* about their emotional process that they do not make time for simple enjoyment of life. Everything can be a deep and heavy issue. Families can get burdened by constant emotional communication.

6. Can be so *absorbed in their creative endeavors* that they completely neglect the practical side of life, such as producing an income, making meals, maintaining a household, yard, and automobiles.

7. *Expect their spouses to be as romantic, sensitive, and expressive of feelings as they*, expectations that no other type can live up to.

DISCUSSION 5. *Are you or is your spouse an NF? Discuss whether the lists describe some important aspects of your personality. Do you recognize one of your children or parents as an NF?*

DISCUSSION 6. *What is it like to live with an NF spouse? How does NF behavior affect the family? What special contributions are made to your family by the NF partner?*

Nate is an NF. You would not think of him as "romantic" in the classic sense because he does not send me flowers or like to celebrate Valentine's Day. But, he is warm and expressive of his appreciation of me. He only gives cards when they are called for, but they melt my heart. He enjoys dreaming up adventures for us. I have learned that his fantasies motivate and enliven him and are not to be taken literally—like the one about making love on an airplane! His fantasies can be modified to take into account available resources. Before I learned that about him, I was fearful that he would actually carry out ideas that seemed unrealistic to me.

Nate is excited about participating in the professional growth of his clients, and he establishes close friendships with them. He finds out all about their families and frequently dines in their homes when consulting out of town. He is really *interested* in them. As an organization consultant he gets in the middle of interpersonal problems and helps adversaries learn to work together. He believes that people can make a better world and does not hesitate to share his philosophy. He is so convincing that he brings out the best in people.

The NT Temperament

NTs are a combination of the iNtuitive imagination and the Thinking type's rational, logical mind. NTs, about 12 percent of the population, hunger for competency and mastery over their world. They love to talk about their ideas about how systems or people work. Competence is so important to them that they may seem arrogant, but they are more self-doubting than the other types. Skills with people do not come naturally, so they may need help from family members in making emotional and personal contact. They are eager learners, but must be approached with respect rather than criticism. They get defensive and argumentative when they think they are accused of being wrong. They need opportunities to share their intellectual curiosity and prowess with their families. They enjoy the companionship of an equal relationship rather than status or prestige.

NTs' interests lead them to fields of science and research, inventing, and leadership of groups in careers such as business, military, and medicine. They are good teachers if they consider the learner's needs. In marriage, they are good systems planners (how four people can use the shower in the morning and everybody be on time) and good disciplinarians if they consider the child's emotional needs. Women NTs have difficulty because the natural dominance of the NT, combined with interests in areas that are not typical for women, is often viewed as unfeminine.

When NTs are at their best, they:

1. *Create systems* in a family or organization so that the family or organization can function in an orderly manner. They are eager to improve on these systems and will embrace change enthusiastically once they can see the logic in it. They are inventors and embody the General Electric motto, "We bring good things to life."

2. Love to *learn and teach* anything. They can create stimulating conversation about anything.

3. Make decisions after *an analysis of information* from many points of view. They research decisions, for instance, by checking *Consumer Reports* before buying anything, and consult several medical references before making a decision affecting their health.

4. Are compelled by their self-critical nature to *keep learning and growing*, although they are unlikely to share their self-doubts with other people.

5. Are able to *speak the truth as they see it*, even when the truth is difficult to say.

6. Are *natural leaders* because of their ability to sift through details, get to the heart of the matter, and convince others of what is important. As a result they rise to the top in industry, science, and academia.

7. Are able to *function in a negative, critical environment*. They do what they think is right regardless of the obstacles.

8. Are appreciated by spouses for their level-headed ability to make *plans to accomplish family goals, their intelligent conversation, and their creative problem solving.*

When their strengths are carried too far, NTs:

1. Create systems that have *no practical value* to anyone else.

2. Can be so absorbed in projects of their own that they *ignore emotions in themselves and others.* Intellectual snobs, they can be impatient with family members and others whom they view as incompetent or stupid.

3. May *collect so much information* that decisions become convoluted and more complex than is necessary.

4. Can be *so self-critical* that they immobilize themselves. Self-criticism can also be directed to criticism of others, creating a negative, stressful environment for a family.

5. Can be *offensive* with their statements of truth as they perceive it because they fail to take into account the receiver's feelings.

6. Can be *dominant and stifling* in insisting that things be done their way. This prevents others from being creative or expressive. NTs believe in their own rightness and easily convince others they are right. Spouses will suddenly leave an NT because the NT has not been listening to another point of view, and the NT will be completely surprised because he or she was "right" instead of being loving.

7. May see a *negative, critical environment as normal* and not recognize the stress it creates in their own bodies and in the lives of other people.

8. Have spouses who complain about *their lack of expression of affection and other feelings,* their arrogance, and their dominance.

DISCUSSION 7. *Are you or is your spouse an NT? Discuss whether the lists describe some important aspects of your personality. Do you recognize your child or your parent as an NT?*

DISCUSSION 8. *What is it like to live with an NT spouse? How does NT behavior affect the family? What special contributions are made to your family by the NT partner?*

Ariana and I are NTs. We are unusually sensitive and cry easily in sentimental moments. However, we do not use our feelings to make decisions. Our judgment overrides our feelings. This gives us the discipline to accomplish whatever we set out to do. She sticks to her vegetarian diet in the face of all temptation. I stick to my weight maintenance plan. We spend money in a disciplined way. I studied to produce academic excellence while my friends were having more fun. She has worked long hours on a theater set while her boyfriend complained about her absence. Both of us have had difficulty in relating to men because many men expect women to be more nurturing and compliant than is our tendency. We tell the truth as we see it and let the chips fall. Fortunately I found a man who is strong enough to see through my criticalness to the tender inner core. Ariana is still young, but the twig is bent. I hope that she will be more self-aware than I was and therefore more efficient in finding a compatible partner, but we both know there will be inherent problems for her, too.

My NT personality serves me well as a psychologist. I use my analytical mind and curiosity to understand every aspect of human behavior. Because competence is so important, I strive hard to help clients find solutions to their problems. Although I am sympathetic, I urge them to face issues that are difficult for them. I do not withdraw from powerful emotions. I know I am not the therapist for all clients. Some people want a warm person who will show *caring* about their emotions more than I can.

Are You Happy with Your Type?

People are usually happy with their type if they are feeling loved at home and successful at work. If you can understand yourself and appreciate what you offer, you can help someone else appreciate you. You can also interpret conflicts in a way that respects everyone involved rather than discrediting another. For example, Nate initially felt my requiring the children to obey certain rules was unloving. I thought he was so tolerant that the children would not learn self-discipline. Each of us could argue with psychological expertise supporting obedience to rules and loving acceptance, but the arguments left walls between us. When we learned about our preferences and temperaments, we were able to talk about our differences in a way that respected both of our styles rather than insisting that one of us must be wrong.

Other people's disappointment in your type can create disappointments in the relationship, and can influence you to think there is something wrong with your natural type. A spouse or a boss may want a person with qualities that are not natural for your type. Although people can learn the skills that are natural for another type, you will feel most comfortable with the behavior typical of your type. Most people want to be more effective, but they don't want to change their personalities or Myers-Briggs types. When people think of changing themselves, they usually think about becoming more balanced, such as, "I'd like to be more sensitive," or "I'd like to be more outgoing." They do not consider becoming a personality opposite to themselves. Learning to balance yourself with opposite-type behavior is discussed in the next chapter.

If you are very disappointed with your type and are unwilling to notice the benefits of being you, you may have grown up with a parent who was different from you and who did not appreciate your natural traits. If your disappointment in yourself is a problem for you, find a counselor who can affirm you and help you overcome your parents' messages.

To some extent most people think their own behavior is the natural way to be. We compare others with ourselves and think there must be something wrong with them. But sometimes people are *too* happy with their type. They become upset and critical of others who are different. Thinking or communicating that you are right all the time causes distress in a marriage. It will help such people to recognize that they are not the only example of "normal" and that other kinds of people can get along very well doing things in a different way.

DISCUSSION 9. *What special benefits does your marriage have as a result of your temperaments? What problems does your marriage have have as a result of your temperaments?*

DISCUSSION 10. *Discuss couples you know. What benefits and problems do you notice as a result of their temperaments?*

In the next chapter you will practice talking about yourselves in a way that will lead you to appreciate each other and live more harmoniously with differences. It will help you understand the natural effects of your personalities on your marriage. You will think about how to compensate for what is missing and balance those preferences that are too strong.

For Practice

Recall a time when there was frustration or conflict between you and your spouse. Discuss with your spouse how your personality types might have contributed to the frustration. Remember a time when you were feeling especially good about each other. How did your personality types contribute to the feelings of harmony?

NOTES

1. David Keirsey and Marilyn Bates, *Please Understand Me* (Del Mar, Calif.: Prometheus Nemesis Book Co., 1984).

2. Isabel Briggs Myers, *Gifts Differing* (Palo Alto, Calif.: Consulting Psychologists Press, 1983).

3. Statistics about population composition are from Keirsey and Bates, *Please Understand Me*.

Chapter Five

Appreciating Differences

In chapters 2–4, we examined aspects of identity, what makes us individuals. This chapter explores ways couples can use strengths and balance differences in order to ease tension and inspire cooperation. Couples working in a group will get to know other couples of similar and different types and begin to use them as resources and models for solving conflicts between types. Couples studying alone are encouraged to think about the marriages of friends and relatives to broaden their understanding of how different people interact.

Creating Harmony

The period of unconditional love varies with each couple, but it always ends. After the honeymoon is over, most couples try to change each other. Often they do this by criticizing the other's personality as though that person could actually become another type if he or she simply wanted to. The change from acceptance and adulation to irritation and criticalness occurs gradually but insidiously. Young couples, for example, often carve out territory in order to avoid conflict. Wives typically take responsibility for household care and children; husbands often take on the finances, the cars, and the yard. After several years of marriage, these traditional couples may become dissatisfied with such territorial decisions. One spouse may object to how the other is managing his or her domain—a husband may complain about his wife's housekeeping or a wife about the unavailability of money. Some couples live with each other for many years without complaining and suddenly feel intolerant or irritated with the other because the unspoken discontent has become impossible to ignore. Not having the skills to identify and manage the real differences in personal style frequently leads to marital breakdown and divorce. By understanding Myers-Briggs personality types, couples can work together to develop creative approaches to problems instead of attacking each other.

Appreciating each other's personalities benefits a marriage in at least three ways. First, appreciation feels good and adds to partners' enjoyment of each other. Second, appreciating each other's differences allows partners to experience the other person as a separate person with his or her own makeup instead of treating a behavior pattern as a plot designed to punish or frustrate. And third, understanding personalities reduces frustration by allowing partners to solve the problems caused by their differences instead of trying to change the partner's personality. For example, when an extroverted husband gets caught up working the crowd at a party instead of sitting near his introverted wife, a typical response might be accusatory and defensive, such as, "If you cared at all about me you would pay more attention to me at parties," followed by a counterattack of, "Well, if you cared at all about me, you would be happy to go to parties and support me. You know that socializing is necessary for my career." But they can learn to understand this behavior as reflecting a difference in preference. The couple can then have a conversation about how to handle the differences rather than hurling accusations. The problem has nothing to do with caring. It is a difference in preference, which can be solved without insult and argument.

In this chapter I will not teach you how to change your spouse into a different type, but will instead allow you to affirm the strengths of your types and enlist each other's cooperation when those strengths are carried too far. After all, many of us selected our partner *because* of those special qualities that are causing a problem now. I really liked Nate's warm, easygoing, accepting nature before we were married. I should not have been surprised when he was the same warm, accepting parent with his strong-willed son. But, yes, I was as surprised as every other newlywed that our differences turned up as conflicts.

The most important thing to remember in dealing with your spouse's differences is, *don't take the behavior personally.* It is normal for partners to think they are causing their spouse's upsetting behavior. As you learned in the previous chapters, your spouse behaves in a particular pattern partly because of his or her preferences. If you believe your spouse would be different if he or she loved you more, respected you more, or appreciated you more, you lose your power to handle the situation effectively. Your spouse's behavior pattern *is not about you.* For example, a preference difference that is often obvious is the one of Thinking/Feeling, and it is frequently the husband who has Thinking preference and the wife who has Feeling. Thinking types are critical. It gives them their ability to be competent in analyzing everything—the stock market, science, people, business, medicine. However, when that analytical ability is turned on you, as it always will be in a marriage, you must not think it is because you are a terribly flawed person. It is simply your spouse responding to you in the way he or she responds to the rest of the world. (Handling complaints or criticism is discussed in chapter 8.)

But don't think that such problems work in only one direction. A Feeling preference spouse will create problems for a Thinking preference spouse by being unusually sensitive to hurt and rejection. Thinking spouses enjoy their Feeling partner's warm, affectionate, expressive nature most of the time. The Feeling partner's hurt feelings are not the spouse's fault. People with Feeling preference respond naturally to criticism or temporary rejection with strong feelings of hurt. (How to handle emotions is covered in chapters 6 and 10.)

Combinations of Preferences Affect a Marriage

For every couple there are three possible combinations of preferences. Any of the three combinations has the potential for creating harmony or conflict, depending on the skill of the couple in handling it.

In the first combination, the couple shares a preference and the opposite preference is missing. I discuss this below in "Compensating When Your Marriage Lacks a Preference." When partners enjoy similar activities and avoid others, they will often be highly compatible at first. Rapport comes naturally. However, over the years, their relationship will suffer because of the activities they avoided. For instance, two Feeling partners can express love and appreciation because that comes naturally to persons with Feeling preference. They go along with each other to maintain harmony. They may, however, avoid conflicts, never telling each other about problems they are encountering, and build up internal resentments over the years. If one partner had a Thinking preference, that person would be more comfortable and familiar with expressing conflict, because persons with Thinking preference do not consider the other person's feelings as much as persons with Feeling preference.

In the second combination, a couple has some opposite preferences. Such differences can be complementary. There is a possibility for spouses to contribute a variety of skills to balance a relationship. But it is more difficult to feel rapport with and value someone who is different. For example, a wife with a Sensing preference might enjoy tending the lawn and garden. Her husband, being iNtuitive, may not enjoy the details of practical work, but, instead, likes to do things he can think about creatively, such as preparing a gourmet dinner. The differences could create conflict if the wife with Sensing preference is upset about her iNtuitive husband's distaste for doing the work needed to keep the yard beautiful. The effect of opposite preferences is discussed below in "Appreciating Your Spouse's Strengths."

In the third combination, one person's preference is so strong that it is out of balance. This is discussed below in "Balancing a Strong Preference." Any preference carried too far has a negative influence. For instance, a wife may be so strong in Judging that she has everyone in the household regimented and feeling resentful. A husband may be so strong in Perceiving that he rarely schedules anything in advance and procrastinates about all projects. A partner may be so iNtuitive that he or she lives in a fantasy and avoids taking care of the details of reality. This chapter will help couples identify and manage these difficulties.

✔ **EXERCISE 1.**
Refer to table 5-1 when answering the questions below.

Table 5-1. The Eight Preferences

Extroversion	Introversion
Sensation	iNtuition
Thinking	Feeling
Judging	Perceiving

1. **Write your Myers-Briggs types in the blanks. Refer to your journal entry for chapter 2 to refresh your memory.**

   Wife's Myers-Briggs initials_____
   Husband's initials_____

2. **Out of each of the pairs of preferences, which are the same for the two of you?**

3. **If you share a preference, the opposite preference is missing in your marriage. Identify your missing preferences.**

4. **Which preferences in your marriage are opposite?**

In Exercise 2 you will explore some of the effects on a marriage when persons share preferences or have opposite preferences. There are, of course, many other influences on a marriage, such as the skills each partner brings to the relationship, the combination of preferences, and the number of children in a family and their types, not to mention external factors.

✔ **EXERCISE 2.**
1. **Circle in your book the pairs of preferences in table 5-2 that are the same and those that are opposite in your marriage.**

2. **How do your similar preferences affect your marriage? Use table 5-2 for ideas.**

3. **How do your opposite preferences affect your marriage? Expand on the examples and think of some examples of your own.**

Table 5-2. Typical Effects of Similarities and Differences in Preference

Both Extroverts	Both Introverts	An Extrovert and Introvert
Extroverts create a lot of conversation and social activity.	Introverts create fewer distractions and the possibility of a lot of time together.	They may complement each other: the Extrovert may introduce the Introvert to people, and the Introvert may balance the Extrovert's busy life with quiet time at home.
The couple may have difficulty scheduling time alone together.	The couple may not talk enough to exchange information and feelings.	*Or* the Introvert may feel abandoned by the Extrovert's involvement in activities and the Extrovert may feel bored by the Introvert's reluctance to do many things.

Both Sensing	Both iNtuitive	A Sensing and an iNtuitive
Life is action-oriented. Chores are taken care of effectively.	INtuitives create lively conversation. Excitement about ideas abounds.	With mutual respect, one can be the idea person and the other can carry out the action.
Conversation may become boring after a while because it may focus primarily on daily and personal events instead of broader topics.	Excitement can become volatile arguments. Daily chores may be neglected.	*Or* the couple can think that they speak different languages because it is hard for each to appreciate what the other talks about. They can feel bored with each other.

Both Thinking

Both are usually accomplished in their work as well as home maintenance, hobbies, and all other aspects of life.

They may be liberal in their criticalness of everything and not expressive of appreciation and love.

Both Feeling

Both spouses express appreciation, love, and romance. They support and nurture each other.

With little confrontation of conflicts, over time accumulated conflicts can erode the loving feelings.

A Thinking and a Feeling

The couple can provide balance between lively emotion and cool-headed reason.

Or the Feeling person may want the partner to express more love and have more conversation about feelings and relationships. And the Thinking partner may want the relationship to be more "reasonable," being happy when things are running calmly.

Both Judging

Life is managed well. The couple accomplishes a lot at home and at work.

They may be scheduled and serious. If two Judging types have many commitments, they organize and schedule priorities but will likely become tense and exhausted. Relaxation may be neglected.

Both Perceiving

The relationship can be playful and fun. They entertain each other with humor.

They can be disorganized. If a lot of demands are made on a couple, such as with several children in a complex urban community, life can be stressful without organization.

A Judging and a Perceiving

If they have excellent communication, the Judging person can plan and organize while the Perceiving person provides crisis intervention and relaxation with spontaneous, playful events.

Or the Judging person may criticize the Perceiving person for not managing time and belongings. The Perceiving person may, as a result, feel inadequate and stop contributing her or his delightful spontaneous energy.

From this, you may easily see how you are bending to accommodate your spouse in ways that are not natural for you. For example, if your spouse is a stickler for details, you may clean up the kitchen with a lot more precision than if left to your own devices. It may be more difficult for you to notice what your spouse does for you because you may take it for granted. In the example above, if the kitchen is usually clean, you may not notice the work your spouse is doing to clean it. Or in the case of managing money, you may stick to agreed spending limits so that your spouse will feel the security of living with a financial plan, although it is not natural for you. Your spouse may not notice that you support him or her in this way. It helps to point out, from time to time, what you are doing to support your spouse.

Support means providing the opportunity and encouragement for your spouse to do what she or he enjoys. Support may be quite natural for you or may require some effort because you are different from each other. For example, your husband may cooperate with the schedule you, a Judging type, developed for morning showers. Your wife may plan the details of the vacations because planning is not something you, a Perceiver, enjoy. Your wife may make meals for friends, which you, an Extrovert, appreciate. Your husband may give sentimental cards to you, an NF, a romantic.

If you cannot think of any ways in which your spouse supports you, it may indicate a problem with how you perceive your spouse. You might think of a time in the distant past, right before or after your wedding, when you felt the glow of romantic love. You may ask persons who know you well to suggest ways in which your spouse supports you. Ask your older children, parents, siblings, or good friends. They need not know about the Myers-Briggs types. If you talk with these people and you still believe that your spouse is completely unsupportive, seek counseling about how to cope with this.

I can think of many ways I wish Nate would support me. I wish he liked to go to movies more frequently so I would not have to phone someone else to go with me (my Introversion). I wish Nate would put things where they belong (my Judging). I wish Nate would do the gardening so I would not have to do it and could avoid the details and routines that iNtuitives dislike. I wish Nate made more money so we could send the kids to college *and* hire out all the household work (again, the details and routines). Ah, this list comes so easily. In future chapters you will learn how to clarify requests, make promises, and negotiate conflicts, which will help manage some of these differences.

DISCUSSION 1. *Tell each other how you are presently supporting each other.*

DISCUSSION 2. *In what additional ways do you wish your spouse would support you? Share these wishes with each other.*

Compensating When Your Marriage Lacks a Preference

The combination of your preferences—both the preferences you have and those you do not have—affects your marriage. When you as a couple are missing a particular preference, you have the complementary advantages of the preference that you both possess but do not have the advantages of the one that is missing.

When both partners lack a particular preference, they tend to avoid the activities typically enjoyed by persons with that preference. Our lives are made up of activities that require use of each preference, whether the preference is comfortable for us or not. Creating an enjoyable life is an art that involves emphasizing those activities that come naturally and still doing what is necessary but less natural for our type. For example, Nate and I are both iNtuitives, so we are missing the Sensing preference. This means that neither of us naturally enjoys the reality-oriented details of everyday life, such as buying groceries, painting the house, tarring the driveway, or feeding and weeding the roses. Nate recently tried to stop a leak on the kitchen faucet and because of his inexperience, we were without water until the plumber could rescue us. Neither do we have fun with the activities typical of Sensing-type persons. These activities might be decorating the house with matching curtains and wallpaper, packing creative lunches for the kids, putting together a model airplane, coaching sports for the kids or community, or teaching a church school class. It takes some effort and struggle for us to get along without Sensing.

You as a couple will need to develop strategies for compensating for those preferences you do not have. We have learned to get the Sensing activities done without unduly burdening either of us. Nate and I know that attention to details is *really* missing in his personality, so most of the time, I handle the details. For example, I balance the checkbook (with great struggle and effort until I acquired a computer program). I plan the details of vacations (I do not mind this, since vacation plans capture my iNtuitive fantasies). Nate grew up managing cars and does not mind taking care of ours. He takes them for regular maintenance rather than doing the work himself. I am happy to relinquish these activities. Neither of us chooses to spend much time at these practical activities. You can usually tell the houses of iNtuitives by their lack of order and maintenance, unless the iNtuitives have found a way to delegate the tasks. We do not entertain often.

In Exercise 3 you will explore how your marriage is affected by your similarities, which means a preference is absent. Discovering missing preferences will help you identify challenges you face as a couple.

✔ **EXERCISE 3.**
  1. **Identify your missing preferences from Exercise 1.**
  2. **Turn to chapter 3 (pp. 45–51) and review the list of characteristics of the preferences that you are missing.**
  3. **Discuss with your spouse how the absence of a particular preference affects your lives. Table 5-3 may give you some ideas.**
  4. **What are some of the ways you take care of activities that neither of you naturally enjoys? Think of one additional activity you might try in order to compensate for what is missing. Use Table 5-3 for ideas.**

Table 5-3. Compensating for Missing Preferences in a Marriage

If You Are Missing . . .	To Balance the Missing Preference
Extroversion: A social initiator is missing. A couple can get bored with each other because they lack friends and activities. Also, the couple may talk little with each other.	In order to encourage two Introverts to talk to each other, set aside a special time for conversation about your lives with no distractions. Use an agenda or discussion materials. Make a plan for activities that include other people.
Introversion: Quiet reflection alone or together is missing. The couple may be going in the wrong direction and not notice it. They may also burn out.	In order to encourage two Extroverts to set aside time for rest and relaxation, schedule special time each week alone or only with each other. Once they are together, talking will not be a problem.

If You Are Missing . . .	To Balance the Missing Preference
Sensing: The reality factor is missing. Details of daily life such as a budget, house, yard, and car care are avoided. Daily necessities of child care can be resented.	In order to compensate for a missing reality factor, two iNtuitives might admit they dislike housekeeping and cooking, split up the duties evenly, or hire someone else when possible. Routines of child care should be shared, leaving time and energy for both parents for creative play with their children, which iNtuitives enjoy.
iNtuition: Fantasy and possibility thinking are missing. A couple gets discouraged by problems because they cannot see possibilities.	To cope with two Sensing spouses being too limited in their thinking, practice brainstorming solutions to any problem. Include friends and relatives to help brainstorm.
Thinking: Rational, analytical problem solving is missing. Couple may dwell on emotional upset without getting to solutions. Two Feeling spouses want to please each other so much that they cannot say no until they are fed up.	To compensate for two Feeling spouses having too much sympathy, and therefore, being unable to say no, practice saying no to something once a day.
Feeling: Attention to harmony and empathy are missing. Hurts and resentment can go unattended. Appreciation is not provided.	To develop more tenderness in two Thinking spouses, practice giving an affirmation or appreciation once a day (see chapter 7).
Judging: Order and planning are missing. Life can be chaotic, with lots of unfinished projects.	To develop better time management in two Perceiving spouses, you could keep a family calendar of each family members' activities, perhaps on the refrigerator. You have to remember to use it. Have family meetings to decide priorities.
Perceiving: Attending to the present moment is missing, as well as spontaneous play and joy. Life without Perceiving is a burden.	Two Judging-type spouses can plan play time together. Set aside time each week in which you will be together with no goal except the pleasure of your company.

Appreciating Your Spouse's Strengths

When a couple has opposite preferences, their marriage can be balanced by dividing up labor according to who enjoys the task. That is a benefit of their division of preferences. At the same time, they have a strong potential for misunderstanding each other's differences. As a result, spouses with different preferences are often afraid of the partner's strengths. Each feels comfortable with his or her own strengths and is sure the *other* person has a problem. For example, a spouse with Thinking preference may fear the emotions that are comfortable and natural for the Feeling partner. It is normal to fear what is different, so it is important that spouses are educated about the value of the partner's habits and behavior patterns, in order to better understand and appreciate the spouse. There will be less fear and resentment as each understands the other's differences and both develop some ways to compensate.

Couples can develop severe conflicts about the very traits they saw as strengths when they first met. There is truth in that old business about "opposites attract." For instance, you may be a reasonable, clear-thinking sort of person (with a Thinking preference), but life could be dull with another person like yourself. So you are attracted to the emotionally expressive kind of person who laughs and cries easily (a person with Feeling preference), who brings out the love in you. Then you are lucky enough to marry this emotionally expressive person. You discover that your partner makes most decisions based on what will avoid conflict or create a loving relationship. Your spouse is interested in romantic dinners with candles. He or she is not particularly interested in financial plans, job promotions, or how things get fixed. You think your partner does not understand what is important. You wish your partner were more *reasonable*, like yourself.

Couples often divorce over the qualities that attracted them in the first place, as did Jesse and Gail, a couple I treated in marital therapy.

> Jesse is Sensing and Gail is iNtuitive. He is excellent at gathering facts and making decisions relating to those facts. When they married, Gail appreciated Jesse's commitment to financial responsibility and how well he took care of the cars and fixed up the house. Jesse appreciated Gail's imagination. With Gail, he felt anything was possible. They separated because he decided he could support and provide an education for only two children even though it was Gail's dream to have six children. Whenever she would bring up this dream, he would immediately squash it with financial facts.

Actually, this behavior occurred every day in many ways. Whenever Gail, as is typical of iNtuitives, had a fantasy or dream about where to live, what to do on vacation, or how to remodel the house, Jesse stifled all her ideas by telling her they were impractical.

It is essential that each type be able to express those behaviors and experiences typical of their type. The nature of iNtuition is to dream up possibilities. Jesse took each daydream and evaluated it for its practical application. Jesse and Gail were not willing to change their point of view about each other or learn about themselves, and Gail felt so frustrated that she left the marriage. It would have been more effective for Jesse to listen reflectively to Gail so that she could express what children (or her other ideas) meant to her. (You will learn about reflective listening in chapter 6.)

Jesse's difficulty understanding Gail's ideas is not a lot different from Nate's saying he would like to own a manufacturing company and my stifling it with what were obvious facts (to me), outlining our limited finances and ability to buy one. Or Nate's dream of sailing around the world and my pointing out that we do not have a large sailboat or the time, money, or sailing skill.

Fortunately, Nate and I learned to understand our personalities. We are both iNtuitive, but Nate is much more so. We also learned to communicate about this conflict. He told me to let him have his dreams; I was able to understand how important his dreams are to him. He reassured me that he would not jeopardize our financial security with an impulsive decision to buy something before I agreed to it. This was a big relief. Now I can listen to Nate's dreams about owning a company in a way that encourages and supports him. Who am I to say what his limits are or what the future holds?

Partners often recognize what bothers them about their spouse's behavior without noticing that the behavior is beneficial to them some of the time. In the exercise below, you will talk about examples of your spouse's behavior that bothers you, and then see that the behavior has some advantages. For example, Nate waits until the last minute to pack, typical of Perceivers. One summer, I was so overloaded that I did not leave enough time to prepare for our week away on our boat. At the last minute, I asked Nate to handle it. He was happy to run to the store and buy a week's food, throw the necessary kitchen equipment into some boxes, and stuff sheets and blankets into some bags. It would have taken me days!

✔ **EXERCISE 4.**

   1. Write in your journal a criticism of your spouse's behavior.

2. **Consider your comment and then write how your spouse's behavior is a predictable result of his or her Myers-Briggs preferences or temperament.**

3. **Share your list with your spouse.**

4. **Tell your spouse about a time when you benefited from that preference. If you cannot think of any benefits to the preference, ask your partner to help you think of some.**

Balancing a Strong Preference

You or your spouse may be ineffective because you carry a natural preference too far. Obvious dysfunctional behavior such as alcohol abuse or antisocial behavior such as stealing is not a result of a Myers-Briggs strength, and should not be considered in this discussion. Such behavior should be handled in counseling.

People often throw around the word *neurotic*. But what you see as a neurotic trait may simply be a strength that is carried too far and is not effective in the extreme. In fact, all the preferences and temperaments become ineffective if they are extreme and out of balance. For example, Ron is a very strong NF. His strength is warm, supportive, emotional expression. He is friendly and likable. But he wants to be in love all the time, and his warm, good-natured personality carries him too far. If he does not feel in love with his current partner, he looks for a partner for whom he can have those feelings. He avoids the parts of a relationship that make him uncomfortable, such as negotiating conflict. Instead, when conflict gets in the way of his romantic feelings, he moves on to another partner. Ron needs to learn to be practical, a Sensing trait, and to address inevitable conflicts in relationships, a Thinking trait, in order to have a lasting relationship. Achieving balance is a learning process.

Nate, a Perceiver who likes to do things at the last minute, is an officer in the Army Reserve. His strength is getting things done only as needed, which works well in a crisis with a short-term objective. This process does not work with long-range goals. He has to accomplish a certain amount each year to get points for retirement. He chose to develop a manual for training leaders. The deadline was last week. He had planned to spend the whole week working on it. After much of the week had passed, he planned to spend the last two days on it. Finally, on the last day he scrambled to do a year's work in one day. He ended up rescheduling the deadline. The challenge for Perceivers is to break down long-range goals into small segments and set time limits. Nate's loathing of scheduling his work in advance—a trait typical of those with a Perceiving preference—resulted in his waiting too long.

In order to be more effective you will need to learn from the opposite preference and perhaps try some new behavior. You can learn to be more effective for the rest of your life by following certain steps:

1. You have to be willing to admit that you need balance. Identify which preference you carry too far and the opposite one you need to learn. Be aware of the problem behavior and preference in detail. Write a few examples of incidents when your preference was carried too far. For example, if you are an organized Judging type who likes to know exactly what is going to happen at all times, you may get upset when things do not go as you expected or scheduled.

2. Write the name of at least one person you know with the preference you wish to learn. Write how that person might handle the examples you named in step 1. For instance, using the example in step 1, you may have a Perceiving sister who is relaxed and flexible. You will never become like her, but you may be able to take some tips from her that can help you be more flexible.

3. Discuss the preference you want to learn with people in your life so that you learn about it in more detail. Tell your family what you are working on. They will help you. For example, you might say, "I'm trying to lighten up and be more flexible and spontaneous." Tell them to encourage you but not to criticize you.

4. Practice using the preference in small steps. For instance, in learning to be more flexible you might try considering your child's impulsive request instead of saying no immediately.

In what follows, you will be talking about how your own type may have been a problem for you. It is very important that each spouse listen uncritically, even though the preference discussed may involve an area of conflict for him or her. This discussion entails admission of vulnerability.

✔ **EXERCISE 5.**
   1. **Write in your journal about a situation in which you felt ineffective.**
   2. **Share with your spouse which preference might have been carried too far and therefore might have gotten in your way.**
   3. **Consider how you might have been more effective if you had used the opposite preference for balance.**
   4. **Identify someone from whom you could get some tips about the opposite preference.**

✔ **EXERCISE 6.**

 1. **This is easy: Write in your journal about a situation in which your spouse was ineffective (just one).**

 2. **Which preference might have gotten in the way of your spouse's effectiveness?**

 3. **Discuss with your spouse how she or he might have been more effective with some balance from the opposite preference.**

 4. **What are some tips for being more effective in the future?**

 5. **Both partners choose one change to make in the future to be more effective.**

For Practice

Set aside an hour or more of uninterrupted time to spend with your spouse during the week. During that time, discuss how your opposite preferences add to your relationship and how they create conflict. For example, if you have a Judging preference and your spouse has a Perceiving preference, talk about how your organization and decisiveness contribute to the marriage and how your partner's spontaneous and fun-loving nature contribute to the relationship. During the same conversation, acknowledge how those same differences create conflict.

PART II.
Communicating—It Is Blessed to Give

Give, and it will be given to you. A good measure, pressed down, shaken together, running over, will be put into your lap; for the measure you give will be the measure you get back.
—Luke 6:38

Communicating is giving of ourselves, which is all that we are. *Communication* is the link necessary to integrate two persons with separate identities into a marriage. The kinds of communication that nourish a marriage are listening with understanding, appreciating and affirming your partner, making requests for what you want, making and keeping promises, and expressing your feelings. These communications will increase intimacy and develop a partnership that will bring out the best in each person.

One of the most precious gifts you can give to another is listening without interruption or judgment. In chapter 6 you will learn listening skills, in particular, how to use a process I call "reflective listening." Reflective listening is one of the most powerful communication skills because once you learn the process, you can help your partner talk with you about anything, even innermost feelings. And if you listen, your spouse will then be more receptive to listening to your opinion or feelings.

When we love someone we see the best in that person and tell him or her about it. In chapter 7 you will learn that positive messages make spouses feel good. They tell partners that they understand and value each other, which produces love and goodwill in return.

When we complain, we create static in the lines. The lines of communication must be open and free from noise and distraction for a message to get through. Requests are much more effective than complaints for getting attention and actually making something happen to resolve a problem. No one wants to hear a complainer, so most people stop listening to complaints. Nonetheless, you may need to express your unpleasant feelings to be understood and to identify the request you want to make. In chapter 8 you will learn to turn your complaints into requests. Will you get everything you request? No, but you will get a lot more than if you complain. The first step is to make your wants known in a way that does not turn off your partner's ability to hear.

A partnership requires making and keeping promises, which are essential for trust. Trust is knowing you can depend on your spouse, in big matters, such as fidelity and financial responsibility, and in small ones, such as being home on time. As you look at trust more closely, you will see that you can depend on your partner for some things and not for others. You will learn that trust cannot be assumed. Instead, you must make agreements with your partner, called promises, so that both of you have the same understanding about the agreement. You will learn what to do if promises are not kept, and how to renegotiate promises so that they will be kept.

Feelings are the glue that connect people in a loving relationship. When partners share feelings, they tell each other what is important and meaningful in their lives. The sharing of feelings makes a marriage more intimate than any other relationship. In a loving relationship, partners must express and hear the uncomfortable messages of hurt, disappointment, anger, and sadness as well as appreciation, anticipation, pride, and pleasure. In chapter 10 you will learn how to share feelings constructively.

When partners know themselves and each other enough to appreciate the talents and wisdom that each contributes to the relationship, and when they can communicate with each other constructively, they can continually recreate a relationship with health, vitality, partnership, and love.

Chapter Six

Reflective Listening Creates Miracles

Knowing how to listen reflectively to your spouse is one of the most effective skills in creating intimacy and resolving problems, and yet, in our culture we are not taught how to listen. Instead, we present our own point of view. This chapter discusses the process known as reflective listening, by which you are encouraged to listen to your partner even when you disagree.

Reflective listening is not appropriate, however, in the presence of verbal abuse. Both husbands and wives can be guilty of verbal abuse. Many spouses, who are at other times loving, express their own anger by abusing a partner. Everyone has a personal boundary beyond which he or she feels hurt. This boundary depends on the sensitivity of the person; some people feel hurt more easily than others. But verbal abuse goes beyond hurt feelings. It is characterized by particular behavior: derogatory or swear words used to refer to the spouse; insulting remarks; teasing in a belittling way about a spouse's weaknesses. Verbal abuse damages both persons. Use of alcohol increases the possibility of verbal abuse for some people. If this is happening in your relationship, whether you are the giver or receiver, seek counseling.

The Importance of Reflective Listening

Reflective listening is the most powerful skill a couple can acquire. It can make the difference between a loving bond and alienation. Reflective listening is an essential ingredient in healthy, dynamic, trusting relationships in which feelings of intimacy and sexual expression can flourish. I treated a couple in marital therapy who were so alienated from each other that Susan, the wife, was considering divorce. I recommended a therapeutic separation (a structured separation for the purpose of crisis intervention and learning) as an alternative to divorce, to see if they could buy time, reduce the tension, and learn the skills needed for getting back to the loving feelings they had once shared. For months, Susan told Michael about her feelings about his family, his parenting skills, and his lack of help around the house.

Michael responded predictably each time with a reason for his behavior. Their series of conversations went like this:

Susan: Michael, I feel rejected by your mom. She doesn't talk to me when she calls. She asks for you immediately. She doesn't even ask how I'm getting along.
Michael: Well, you have to understand that she misses me. I was closest to her, and after her divorce, she needs to talk to me.
Susan: She's known me a long time. She could talk to me too. It hurts that she has so little interest in me.

Susan: Michael, you are so critical of the children. I'm really angry about your harsh and stern way with them. I'd like you to be more flexible and understanding so the kids feel loved.
Michael: But you give them everything they want! They need more discipline!

Susan: I feel exhausted at the end of the day. I don't feel like I have a life beyond wiping noses and spills. I'd like you to make meals a few times a week.
Michael: That's your job. I work all day while you get to stay home and do what you want to do. Besides, I take care of the lawn, too. I can't come home and cook.

I worked hard to coach Michael to listen, but to no avail. He was so confident that his point of view was the right one, he could not empathize with his wife. Susan gave up. Michael was deeply hurt and angry at her decision. All he could feel was abandonment. And after all this, Susan said, "Michael could have gotten me to stay if he had listened to me." And she really meant "listen," not "obey," as the word "listen" is often used.

Learning reflective listening has had an impact on Nate's life:

Reflective listening has given me my first exposure to intimacy. It is the vehicle that transcends inherent differences. It has allowed me to be connected at the level of the soul. A soul is the common thing all human beings have. Not sex, color, or height. Listening is one of the greatest gifts you can give another human being. When we take that gift lightly, we lessen the power of relationship with people. It is not a frivolous activity.

It has given me the ability to hear what is *really* being said. I have a fundamental belief that there are no bad people, only people operating out of their histories. Reflective listening gives people the freedom to be nasty, ugly, and emotional. Underneath all of that is their goodness clouded by fears, doubts, and injury. Reflective listening has removed for me fear that surrounds personal upset and conflict. If I listen effectively I can touch the goodness of all people. I have not found an exception to that. The child of God is in everyone.

Reflective listening gives me energy. All I have to be is with the other person. I do not have to be smart or right. I can check out what I am hearing and feel the freedom to risk being wrong. I don't have to fight, or show how smart or dumb I am. That's energizing. My level of energy has exponentially leaped as a result of being a reflective listener. The speaker truly has the answers to the problem. I don't. My opinion is insignificant. My judgments have to be suspended or delayed in order for reflective listening to work. To be a strong evaluator and judger takes a lot of energy. Reflective listening has given me the capacity to be brilliant. People pay me good money, not for what I know, but for how I am with them.

To listen reflectively, you have to start with a belief system about human behavior. It is grounded in a fundamental philosophy that contains an understanding and respect for individual history. What pops up today has a good chance of not having much to do with today and a lot to do with past traumas, pain, and injuries. Reflective listening is a powerful way of accessing the source of what a conflict may be about. It is vitally important to operate from our sources of experience. It is hard to be in the present if we are not connected with the original source. When I listen reflectively, people reach their own understanding of the source of their problem, maybe reexperience the feeling surrounding the problem, and are finished with it.

When someone listens to us, we feel loved. Our feelings of security and self-confidence depend, in part, on our relationship with people who are close to us. If they listen to us and really get our messages, we experience ourselves as important enough to require attention. When someone listens, we are better able to untangle our own thoughts and feelings, so that we can go forward with self-confidence. Should I stay home with the kids another year or should I go to work? Can we really afford to move or would we be better off staying here? Do I want a graduate degree? Should we put Gram in a nursing home or should she live with us? Would spending a year in mission overseas be good for the kids? Life presents an endless array of choices, and we cope much better with them when we talk about them thoroughly with a listening partner.

Reflective listening does *not* mean you necessarily agree with your spouse, a misunderstanding from which many problems arise. In fact, you will usually have to set your opinion aside temporarily in order to empathize with your partner. It requires self-discipline to listen empathetically to something that is upsetting or "not right." I know the benefits of reflective listening, yet I still argue sometimes instead of listening. Most couples do not know how to just listen. And because we are separate human beings, we often have differences of opinion. If our opinion is discounted whenever there is a difference, we can get the mistaken idea that we are not valued or loved. Reflective listening is a way of conveying, "I am present with you and value what you say," in the face of disagreement. The inspiration for setting aside your own opinion in order to listen comes from really believing in the power of listening, and knowing that your turn is coming after your partner feels heard. After the speaker is finished, you can then say what you have been thinking about during the conversation.

It is much easier to listen if you are not being confronted, or do not have a strong stake in the conversation—if, for example, the conversation is about someone else. It is exactly at the moments of personal confrontation, however, that it is most important to use reflective listening. It is at these times that conflict and negative emotional exchanges can be averted. It takes a lot of self-discipline to listen reflectively when you are feeling hurt, but you will experience a payoff in your marriage. In one group a wife wept with relief as she told us that for the first time in twelve years of marriage she had been able to express herself and feel that her husband listened. In another group, after a few months of reflective listening, a wife, Marianne, wrote about the miracle in her marriage. I include her words to motivate you to work at this. Your feelings may be similar to hers.

I was introduced to reflective listening many years ago in Teacher Effectiveness Training. But I shied away from and disliked reflective listening whether as the listener or the speaker. I couldn't accept that reflective listening would truly help my relationship with Larry since I didn't have any firsthand experience that showed me it worked. My experiences were all ones of frustration.

When I refused to listen reflectively and instead defended myself, we had ineffective conversations. As a matter of fact, Larry just wasn't talking to me much. Reflective listening is not an easy or natural process for me. I fight it all the way. When we first went through the training exercises, when it was my turn to use reflective listening, the conversation never got beyond Larry's second statement. Larry kept coming back and saying "No, that's not what I was saying." I just couldn't or wouldn't get his message. To this day

I am not sure if I didn't have the ability to get the message or I just didn't want to get it. Probably a little of both.

At the same time, I was often very frustrated by Larry's reflective listening to me. More than once I asked him to stop reflective listening. I remember a time when I was so frustrated I asked him to just fight with me and stop repeating what I was saying! Of course, he, in true reflective-listening fashion, responded with, "So what I hear you saying is that you would like me to stop using reflective listening and argue with you." The reflective listening continued for a short time until I ended the conversation totally frustrated and angry. I can't remember what the issue was or whether it was ever resolved.

I guess out of desperation since nothing else was working, I started trying to use reflective listening when Larry requested, and I came to recognize my misconception. The problem was not that reflective listening wouldn't work for us. The problem was our inabilities and my unwillingness to do it. The truth is, reflective listening does work. In the last few months I have learned to do it better—at least that's what Larry says. I have found that Larry is much more willing to open up and talk to me. It is a worthwhile process. We have more effective conversations now that we are able to use reflective listening, and Larry is much less frustrated.

I listen reflectively more than I have ever before, but I still get frustrated. It's hard for me to wait until Larry is totally finished to give my reactions or suggestions. Being a person who deals in the immediate, not the future, I am sure I will forget what it is I want to say by waiting until the end. Through practice, hard work, and staying with reflective listening, I have seen that we very well may come to a conclusion that is satisfactory to both of us, and it's okay if I forget a reaction along the way. If it bothers me enough, I will remember.

I have also learned to look at the process, when I am the speaker. At times I am very frustrated by Larry's reflective listening to me, but I am learning to realize that when I feel the need to tell Larry to stop the reflective listening, I must pause and try to figure out what is bothering me. Sometimes, I find Larry has left a state of reflective listening and moved into a state of dominating or directing the conversation. If I point this out to him, he will return to reflective listening and our conversation can continue so I can be heard and feel complete.

Reflective listening has created a miracle in our marriage. Less than a year ago I had strong feelings of indifference toward Larry. I questioned whether I loved him, though I only told this to one other person. That person was not Larry. Over the last few months, as I have successfully used reflective listening, and Larry and others have listened reflectively to me, I no longer question whether I love my husband. I am sure I do. The miracle of reflective listening has recreated love. Miracle is not a word I use lightly. I am a true skeptic of miracles.

DISCUSSION 1. *Tell your spouse about the place of listening in your marriage. What do you feel when your partner listens? What do you feel when your partner interrupts to argue?*

What Is Reflective Listening?

Carl Rogers described reflective listening in 1951 as a way of providing clients with a relationship of acceptance while not intruding on their own ability to explore their feelings.[1] The therapeutic approach was based on the therapist's complete acceptance of the client, understanding the world from the client's point of view. As a disfunctioning person sorted out his or her thoughts in the presence of an accepting therapist, the person naturally developed the ability to "actualize," or develop positive thoughts, solve problems, and benefit the family and community. Listening in a way that reflected emotional meaning was a key ingredient in the therapist's ability to help.

Reflective listening was popularized as "active listening" by Thomas Gordon in *Parent Effectiveness Training,*[2] and has been adapted widely as a communication skill. Gordon took a therapeutic technique and introduced it to the culture as something anyone could learn. He developed a method of teaching parents to listen to their children. The method has since been used in schools and organizations. I prefer to use the Rogers term, "reflective," because that term conveys more accurately what the listener does. I have found that clients and class members understand the process more quickly because the term "reflective" fits the expected behavior.

Reflective listening is not complicated. In fact, there are only seven important points to keep in mind as you learn and implement reflective listening:

1. Reflective listening is putting your partner's message into your own words, including the feelings he or she is conveying. You say back to your partner what you heard. It is *simple to execute.* Anyone who is motivated can learn to do it.

2. Reflective listening is one of the most *powerful communication tools*

because you can always do it to create an effective conversation. You do not have to depend on your spouse to be effective.

3. Reflective listening *clarifies communication*. When two people are exchanging information, there is much room for error in understanding and even hearing. Reflecting back what is said gives an opportunity to correct errors and refine details.

4. Reflective listening *heals wounded and painful feelings*. Everyone experiences hurt and grief from past experiences. When a partner listens to these experiences without evaluation, the wounded spouse heals as a result of the emotional expression.

5. Reflective listening is *useful in quickly defusing emotional conflict*. Anger often escalates when a person anticipates being discredited. Hearing that someone understands is calming.

6. Reflective listening is *difficult to apply* when *really* needed. That is when you are being confronted or your emotional "hot button" is pushed. This takes practice, self-discipline, and motivation.

7. Reflective listening *helps people solve their own problems*. Time and again husbands tell me, "I don't know what to do when she cries, so I try to solve her problem," while wives say with exasperation, "I don't want him to solve my problem; I just want him to *hear* me." When persons with thoughts full of meaning and confusion speak without intrusion (as when someone is listening reflectively to them), they are able to organize their ideas and come to a conclusion themselves. Resolution may not occur immediately, but it will come over time.

When to Use Reflective Listening

In the usual conversation one person speaks, then the second speaks, then the first person speaks again. There is no listener. Of course, each person hears something, but it is never clear what is heard. When the conversation is clear, simple, and free of conflicts, this will be effective most of the time. But many times, often when it is most important, the conversation breaks into arguments or emotional withdrawal because there is no listener.

In your daily conversation, talk as you would normally, until you notice your partner saying something important or with feeling or you are arguing. You do not need to listen reflectively to all your partner's statements. It would probably become annoying. The right time to use reflective listening is when you notice your partner has a strong feeling.

Let your partner speak until finished while you listen. Then roles should change so the listener can speak. Your conversation should have a back-and-forth rhythm. After you practice this for a while, it will become effective and you will do it naturally. And when you recognize you have feelings to express, you can ask your spouse to listen reflectively to you. (How to express feelings effectively is covered in chapter 10.)

Being the Listener

All of us want to get our message across. The most common question that people learning reflective listening ask is, "When will it be my turn to talk?" The answer is, "When the speaker finishes." When you are the listener, you have certain responsibilities:

1. You have internal reactions to cope with. You could react with strong disagreement, excitement, pleasure, anxiety, anger, or a variety of other feelings. If you cannot sympathize with your partner, keep your own feelings on the "back burner" of your mind, or "put them in brackets." You can be sure that you will remember what is important when it is your turn to speak.

2. Intentionally focus on the speaker instead of your own responses. You will learn how to do this in the following exercises.

3. When your spouse pauses, you can ask, "Do you have anything else to say about that?" People love to hear that question because it makes them feel the listener is really available.

4. Notice when your partner has finished. You will know when your spouse has completed a conversation because his or her expression will change from emotional intensity to relaxation. The voice will change dramatically. You will know that reflective listening is one of the most effective responses to a spouse's emotions because you will see your partner's emotions change after they are heard.

When finished, the speaker will often ask, "Well, what do you have to say about that?" Your spouse will have progressed from being unable to hear due to the intensity of his or her own thoughts and feelings to being interested in you. Isn't it worth the wait? When people are finished, they easily acknowledge it.

Some spouses are natural listeners. If you are married to one, you are fortunate. You have enjoyed the benefits of being able to express yourself without interference. It is important that your partner also benefit from your listening, even though it may be a challenge for you to learn.

Provide your spouse the gift of your listening when you have completed your message and have been heard.

The Steps to Reflective Listening

We have all felt frustrated with conversations like this one between Jack and Sarah:

Conversation 1

Sarah [in a disapproving tone]: I noticed you spent $145 at the Wholesale Store yesterday.

Jack [with resentment]: Look! You have control of the checkbook all the time! I'd like to buy what we need sometime.

Sarah [getting angrier]: You know I was saving that money for groceries. You know we're on a tight budget and you can't just go spending money on unessential things! You always spend the money that I save! You're not responsible!

Jack [self-righteously]: I make money and I should have some opportunity to use it. I'm not nearly as irresponsible as you. You spent a huge amount of money on one haircut. How much was that haircut anyway?

Jack and Sarah walk away in frustration or start yelling, as though increased volume increases the likelihood of being heard.

Sound familiar?

Sarah and Jack are having a difficult conversation because each one is accusing the other. If either had been able to listen, they could have had a satisfying conversation. Reflective listening may seem easy to do because the technique is simple. The difficulty comes in getting yourself to do it when you need to. Basically it involves paraphrasing the speaker's message and reflecting back whatever feeling or emotional meaning the speaker is conveying. When you are skilled in reflective listening, you can use it gracefully in conversation without another person knowing a "technique" is being used. It may seem awkward at first, but it is effective even when awkward.

Every conversation has two parts: the content and the emotional meaning. The *content* is the factual part of the message. The *emotional meaning* is the feeling conveyed about what the message means to the speaker. For example, if Nate says with enthusiasm, "The sun's out and the wind's about fifteen knots," the content is the facts conveyed about the sun and the wind. Hearing his enthusiasm and knowing Nate, the emotional message I'd notice is that he is *excited* about going sailing.

You will learn reflective listening in two stages; the examples illustrate progression in learning. First, you will be listening only for content and then you will be including the emotional meaning with the content.

Listening for Content in the Message

When you listen for content, you pay attention to the facts your partner is telling you. For the moment, ignore the feelings that are being communicated; you will notice feelings in the next step. In Conversation 2, below, Sarah initiates the conflict while her husband, Jack, reflects the content. Sarah talks and Jack feeds back only the content after each sentence, as you will be instructed to do. Then, in Conversation 3, they change roles, as you will, and Jack speaks while Sarah reflects what Jack has said. Reflecting only the content will seem awkward. It is not how people normally listen reflectively. However, going through the process in small steps will allow you to learn the technique and be more graceful in future steps. Read the example aloud together before having your own conversation.

Conversation 2

Sarah [with disapproval]: I noticed you spent $145 at the Wholesale Store yesterday.

Jack [reflecting content]: You thought I spent a lot of money at the Wholesale Store.

Sarah [sounding worried]: Yes. We have another week to go in the month.

Jack [reflecting content]: We won't get a check for another week.

Sarah [very concerned]: We may run out of money for groceries.

Jack [reflecting content]: You think we may run short on money for groceries.

Sarah [upset]: You always do this to me. You know we've maxed out our charges. Last paycheck you bought new exercise equipment. When are we going to get in control of our budget?

Jack [reflecting content]: It seems to you that I overspend a lot. You want us not to spend too much. I bought exercise equipment last month and you don't think we can afford it.

Sarah [calmer]: I would not mind it if we stayed on our budget and did not have so much credit card debt.

Jack [reflecting content]: You wouldn't care if I bought exercise equipment if we didn't have high credit card bills.

Conversation 3

Jack [wistfully]: We do not have much fun together any more.

Sarah [reflecting content]: You would like to do more fun things together.

Jack: Well, yes. I remember when we were first married we had great trips together. Remember that camping trip in Canada?

Sarah [reflecting content]: You have fond memories of how our lives used to be.

Jack [a little sad]: You seem tired all the time now. You have one kid nursing and the other one hanging onto your leg. I don't see a place for me.

Sarah [reflecting content]: You notice how involved I am with the kids and you don't feel a part of my life.

Jack: We haven't gone out together in a long time. Have we been out alone since the baby was born?

Sarah [reflecting content]: You can't remember the last time we were out alone.

Jack: I'm afraid we'll grow apart unless we do things together. I like having kids, but I want a marriage, too. That's why I married you.

Sarah [reflecting content]: You're really concerned that we'll grow apart. It's really important to you that we have a marriage separate from being parents.

✔ **EXERCISE 1.**

As you begin to learn reflective listening it is normal to feel awkward and self-conscious. You will feel more natural as you learn to include your feelings. For this exercise have a conversation with your spouse that continues for three minutes, just to learn the method and without getting into an argument. Set an alarm or egg timer for three minutes. Your conversation will not be complete when you stop, but the object of this exercise is to learn reflective listening. You can complete the conversation later.

1. *Wife speaks.* **Choose a topic that is important and meaningful to you. Speak about your topic, one sentence at a time. Make your sentences fairly short. This is not a memory exercise. If your husband does not give correct feedback on what you mean, restate what you said. Do not be critical of his efforts.**

2. *Husband listens.* **Listen to your wife's message and feed it back to her in your own words after one or two sentences. Stay true to what she is really saying. Do not read anything into the message or analyze it. If you change the meaning from what she intended, she will simply correct you. Keep**

repeating what you hear until she feels understood, and go on with the conversation.

3. *Now change roles.* **Husband, speak about a topic that is important to you as your wife listens. Your topic may be entirely different from your wife's topic previously or it may follow up your wife's topic. Repeat the exercise above. Wife, put your husband's message into your own words and feed it back after one or two sentences. This conversation should continue about three minutes.**

DISCUSSION 2. *What was your experience listening and reflecting your spouse's message? What worked well? What difficulties did you have? What did you notice when you were the speaker?*

Listening for the Feelings

Reflective listening includes feeding back emotions in addition to content. When you reflect emotions, your partner will go into the topic in more depth and will express feelings that need to be released. This will feel more natural to both of you than just feeding back content. Usually it is most helpful to include both parts of a message in your feedback. It helps organize the speaker's thoughts so that he or she can think of more details or feelings to add. If, for example, a wife said in a disappointed tone, "Mom won't baby-sit tomorrow," you can feed back the content and feeling message by saying, "You're disappointed that your mom doesn't want to baby-sit tomorrow." If the speaker has a lot to say and is not leaving much room for you to reflect, you can feed back a few words or simply the feeling instead of the entire message. In this example about baby-sitters you could say, "You seem upset." However, most of the time it is more helpful to the person speaking if most of the message is reflected.

To reflect feelings, you must become aware of your partner's feelings. Being aware of feelings is natural for people with a Feeling preference. However, persons with Thinking preference may not notice them until they are intense and unavoidable. If you do not normally notice feelings, tell yourself, "Look for the feelings," whenever someone is speaking to you. Practice it until it becomes a habit.

You can become aware of your partner's feelings in a number of ways.

One way—the easiest—is to receive a direct message, for instance, when our partner tells us, "I really liked it when you offered to give me a back rub." Another way is to observe your partner's tone of voice, facial expression, and body posture. Or you can remember how your partner felt in a similar situation. Or you might imagine how you would feel in the situation, although many of us respond differently to the same situation, making this method unreliable.

As you try to become aware of your partner's feelings, *stick to the immediate observations*. Do not analyze your partner's feelings or give reasons for them. Analysis interrupts the conversation and frustrates the speaker. In the baby-sitting example, analysis would be saying something like, "You're disappointed that your mom can't baby-sit tomorrow because you think she doesn't love you." Another example of analysis would be making reference to the past, such as, "You're angry with me because your mother was so dominating." Avoid the "because" unless your partner tells you reasons for his or her feelings. If you listen reflectively, your partner will tell you any past memories that are related.

Some people are very subtle in their expression of feelings. When such a person is angry, for example, a corner of his mouth may twitch or his facial tone may harden, but there may be no other indications. Or when this kind of person is happy, her eyes may twinkle and she may smile ever so slightly. It is just as important to listen reflectively to persons who give subtle cues as to persons with obvious emotions, but you will need to be more observant. Nonexpressive persons may anticipate that their feelings will not be accepted, and withhold them to avoid conflict. If you accept those feelings and reflect them, your partner can learn over time that it is safe to express feelings. Many wives *say* they desperately want their husbands to tell them what they feel, but when the husbands bring up unpleasant feelings, the wives do not want to hear them. What these wives really mean is, "Tell me your feelings of love and appreciation." In order for a spouse to feel safe in expressing emotions, all of them must be heard, not just the pleasant ones.

You will be inaccurate sometimes as you feed back your partner's feelings. This is to be expected. Your spouse will be so pleased that you are attempting to listen that he or she will be patient when clarifying the meaning of the messages. He or she will simply tell you the feeling that was intended and continue the conversation smoothly. The objective is to facilitate the speaker's expression, not for the listener to be right.

DISCUSSION 3. *Tell your partner how you know what he or she is feeling.*

The sample conversation that follows is a replay of Sarah's conversation as Jack reflects both her message and her emotions. Read it aloud.

Conversation 4

Sarah: As I was saying, we may run out of grocery money before the end of the month.

Jack [listening reflectively]: You think we may not have enough money for groceries before payday and you feel concerned about that. (Here, he fed back the feeling of concern.)

Sarah: Yes. You spend money without looking at the checkbook.

Jack [listening reflectively]: I don't know how much money we have before I write a check, and it worries you that I might spend too much without taking care of the essentials. (He fed back worry, and her following remark indicated he was right. He might have said, "It *frustrates* you that I might spend too much money." If he was incorrect, she would simply tell him that she was really feeling *worried*, and continue her conversation.)

Sarah [with relief in her voice]: Yes! Why do you do that, anyway?

Jack [listening reflectively]: You're glad that I heard your concern and are wondering why I spend money that's needed for groceries. (It is appropriate, here, for Jack to answer Sarah's question.) I spent the money on things we needed at the Wholesale Store, on fertilizer, toilet paper, light bulbs, a couple of shirts, underwear. It's not like I was blowing it. Things are cheaper there. I didn't know we were almost out of money.

At this point, Sarah has felt heard and wants to hear Jack's point of view. Notice how she is more interested in Jack's point of view here, in contrast to the first conversation, on page 97. The reflective listening has allowed both persons to focus on the problem instead of attacking each other. In the natural flow of conversation, Jack would now tell his point of view while his wife listened reflectively. If she has an opinion and feelings about what Jack tells her, she needs to postpone expressing herself until Jack has had his turn to talk.

In Conversation 5, Jack and Sarah change roles. Jack continues his conversation, while Sarah reflects his message and emotions. Read aloud the conversation between Jack and Sarah.

Conversation 5

Jack: I think you're enjoying being a mother so much that you don't think about me the way you used to.

Sarah: You notice how much I enjoy being with the kids and you feel hurt that I'm not as enthusiastic about being a wife. (She suspected he was feeling hurt about her waning enthusiasm for the relationship.)

Jack: Well, I don't know if I'd call it "hurt." Maybe I feel a little "neglected." (He changed the feeling to "neglected.")

Sarah: You feel a bit neglected that I seem so content to take care of the kids. (When you are corrected, simply acknowledge the corrected feeling and continue the conversation. The process is working here.)

Jack: I offer to put the kids to bed, but you want it done only your way. I have some ideas about putting the kids to bed, but you don't listen to me. So I don't even help out with the kids.

Sarah: You feel a little resentful that your ideas are not included in taking care of the kids, so you don't offer to help. (She noticed Jack's resentment.)

Jack: Yes. I think we should let Peter cry in his room more at bedtime. You let him come downstairs for water and juice until very late at night. He'll never learn to go to sleep early.

Sarah: You would really like for me to put Peter down and let him cry instead of letting him come downstairs. You're afraid he won't learn to go to bed on his own. Perhaps you have been feeling frustrated about Peter going to bed late. (Sarah reflected Jack's concern and frustration.)

Jack: Well, yes, I have. (He validated that she heard him correctly.) It would give us a little time together, too, if we could get the kids to bed early. Would you be willing to try that? (Here Jack completed expressing his feelings by making a request.)

Sarah: You really like to spend more time together in the evenings, and would like for us to try letting Peter cry. I would feel more comfortable if I call the pediatrician and ask her opinion. If she says we wouldn't be hurting Peter, I'll try it. (Sarah reflected Jack's request and made an alternative offer, to check it out with the pediatrician first. This completes the conversation.)

Notice that the conversation flowed from one topic to another. As Sarah continued to listen without jumping in to justify herself, Jack was able to get to the bottom of his issue and make a request. Sarah acknowledged the request and then modified it to one that she could accept with more comfort. Reflecting what a spouse has said may seem contrived in these written conversations—but the process works: it clarifies information, allows the speaker to feel understood, and prevents arguments.

✔ **EXERCISE 2.**
   This exercise involves a conversation that is a little more complicated and intimate than the conversation in Exercise 1. You will listen not only for the content of the message but for its emotional meaning.

1. *Wife speaks:* Go back to the conversation begun in Exercise 1 and continue it, or, if it was complete, select another topic, perhaps one that means more to you. Again, keep sentences fairly short.

2. *Husband listens reflectively:* This time try to be aware of your wife's underlying feelings as she is communicating her message. Feed back the content plus the emotional meaning after every sentence or two. Stop after five minutes.

3. *Now change roles.* Husband, you speak now and your wife will reflect back your message and the feelings. Stop after five minutes.

DISCUSSION 4. *What was your experience when your spouse listened reflectively to your feelings? What was your experience as a reflective listener? What else did you notice?*

Responding to Intense Feelings

There are times in everyone's life when intense feelings occur. A person may express joy over an accomplishment, grief over a loss, anger about something that feels threatening, intense disappointment, or fear of harm to the self or a loved one. Events that commonly cause intense feelings are the birth of a child, children beginning school or leaving home, moving, death of a parent or child or other important family member, serious illness, and loss or change of a job.

If you are able to respond to each other effectively during these times, the bond between you will grow stronger. If you do not respond effectively, the spouse with the intense experience will feel isolated and lonely. Reflective listening conveys to the speaker exactly what the partner understands and tells the speaker she or he is not alone.

The person expressing feelings may begin slowly, testing out whether the message is being accepted. As you listen reflectively, your spouse may express more detail about the emotional event that is bothering him or her. As your spouse continues to talk and be heard, he or she will calm down. For significant events, the feelings will be expressed over days and weeks. When people express feelings to someone who understands, it is healing, and as people continue to express themselves, they often arrive at a problem-solving conclusion themselves, without advice. After your spouse has completed expressing feelings, he or she is usually more open to exploring options for action.

You may, nonetheless, be tempted to try to fix your partner's problem to make the pain go away. When strong feelings are involved, you cannot make the problem go away because usually those kinds of feelings are about something that is not easy to fix. Your partner will need to live with the problem for a while before he or she knows the appropriate action to take. Your listening presence can be extremely helpful.

Many couples break up because one endured an intense experience of loss and felt alone. A partner may withdraw into work or silence, and the other can interpret the withdrawal as rejection. Affairs may start as a distraction from the emotional pain. There is more damage to recover from if a couple does not share their pain for a long time.

Marie and Greg learned to communicate and draw closer during a stressful time. Marie lost a satisfying job because her company downsized. She was hired for two other jobs but lost those as well, each time due to her difficulty in performing her job satisfactorily. She was humiliated and sad, but said very little. Her husband, Greg, was a great problem solver and gave her a lot of advice about finding work or coping with unemployment. Greg's advice frustrated both of them. Marie could not use his suggestions because she had so much shame trapped inside. One night they were lying in bed and Marie said, "I don't have any family left." Greg recognized that Marie was alienated from her only brother and was not in touch with other family members. He was her only support, and it was not enough. But because Greg did not know what to say to help her, he did nothing except go to sleep. Greg had learned enough in therapy to know he should have listened reflectively. He went back to the conversation the next day and asked Marie about her feelings:

Greg: Marie, you seemed very sad and lonely last night when you said you do not have any family left. I'd like to hear more about your feelings.

Marie: Well, it's pretty simple. Mom and Dad are gone. Uncle Peter has never been a part of our family. You know we've never had any contact with my cousins. Your family may be goofy, but everybody wants to be together. They celebrate events with each other. There's nobody to care about *me* except you.

Greg: You feel sad because you don't have family members to talk to. You seem a bit envious of my goofy family.

Marie: I have felt so awful about losing my job. My work was all I had. I'm such a burden to you. I should have other people to talk to, but I don't.

Greg: You don't want to burden me, so you wish you had some other people to talk to.

Marie: Yeah. That's how I feel.

Greg's listening allowed Marie to open up and express how she was feeling. When she finished, it was his turn.

Greg: I don't feel at all burdened by you. I wish I could help, and I feel frustrated seeing you sad all the time.

Marie: You seem to be mad at me and push me a lot.

Greg: I just want to help you.

Marie: So your frustration is about not being able to help me?

Greg: Yes, of course. I thought you knew that. I'm surprised that you think I feel like you are a burden.

Marie: When you listen to me, I feel better. I'd like you to do that more often.

Greg and Marie's marriage grew closer and stronger from dealing with the adversity of Marie's job losses once they were able to share their feelings and listen.

Even when you have done something to trigger intense emotions in your spouse, reflective listening is the most effective response. But it is when you feel accused that you will want to do something else: say you didn't mean it, say your partner misunderstands your intention, explain why you did what you did, tell your partner that you are angry too. All of these natural impulses are ineffective. Your partner will continue to feel the intense emotions until he or she is heard. These emotions will be a barrier between you until they are expressed.

Once again, what do you do when your partner expresses strong feelings?

1. *Listen reflectively.*

2. *Listen reflectively.*

3. *Listen reflectively.*

4. *Listen reflectively.*

5. *Listen reflectively.* (At this point you have probably caught on that reflective listening is the only thing to do when someone shares feelings with you.)

6. When your partner has finished expressing, *express your own feelings.*

7. Once you complete sharing, your conflicts may have dissolved or you may have an issue to live with for a while. Some conflicts require several conversations over weeks or months to resolve.

Sharing feelings is not a conflict-resolution process or a problem-solving process. Those processes, however, go more smoothly after sharing.

You may find that you have a loving relationship with minimum conflicts. When you have disciplined yourself to listen reflectively to other people's intense emotions, you will discover that you have a surprising amount of interpersonal power. Your spouse will know you are a good listener and appreciate it. You will be trusted with more information and included in the "feedback loop." Your spouse will feel more closely related to you. The open, trusting relationship between the two of you will trickle over into other parts of your life, such as relationships with your children.

Exercise 3 demonstrates how strong emotions can be handled with compassion by reflective listening. You will see how feelings can be healed when they are expressed to an accepting person. In this exercise you will express feelings that are not about your spouse, so that he or she can practice listening to you without the need to argue. The feelings may not arise from a current problem or concern. This would give you an opportunity to share important memories in a way you may not have expressed previously.

✔ **EXERCISE 3.**

1. **Husband, choose a topic that creates strong feelings in you but does not directly relate to your wife. Topics can be about your present life, such as children, where you live, your job, a friend, or something from the past, such as an experience growing up. Wife, listen reflectively to your husband until he is finished expressing his feeling.**

2. **Tell your spouse how the exercise felt to you. If your conversation was lengthy or intense, you may choose to postpone the next part of the exercise until you are fresher. If you postpone it, make sure that you make a date with each other to continue.**

3. **Wife, choose a feeling that you want your husband to understand. The feeling should not directly relate to your husband. Husband, listen reflectively until your wife has finished expressing her feeling.**

4. **Tell your spouse how the exercise felt to you.**

When You Cannot Use Reflective Listening

Sometimes when you are listening reflectively to your partner, the conversation creates so much emotion in you that you cannot listen any longer. Your partner may have said something that created intense feelings in you or you may have so many unresolved issues that whatever your partner says creates strong emotions. When you find it impossible to listen, say so. Ask your partner to listen to you, instead. If your partner agrees, express your thoughts and feelings, and then return to listening to your partner.

This situation works both ways, and you may find that you will want to say something important and your partner will be unable to listen. If he or she interrupts to argue or express something heartfelt, change immediately to reflective listening to your partner. This will allow your partner to say what is disturbing and preventing her or him from listening. Your spouse will probably be able to listen to you after expressing the strong feelings.

At other times, neither of you will be able to listen reflectively. Each of you will try to win the other over to your own point of view without stopping to listen to the other. Do not continue this kind of conversation. Take time out to think and return to the conversation after you feel calmer and *you* can listen.

Motivating yourself to listen reflectively is the most difficult part of the process to learn, but if you believe that reflective listening can make a powerful difference in your marriage, it will be easier. Motivation comes with practice and confidence in the success of the process. Even if you "blow it," as I did in the following conversation, you can always return to your spouse, apologize, and try again.

Reflective listening is easy to do when we are not challenged or stressed, but extremely difficult to apply when we disapprove of our spouse's message. The most important moment to listen is precisely when your partner is feeling something intensely and is in all likelihood disagreeing with you. But at this moment the natural reflex is to give your own opinion. We've all done this. The example that follows, a conversation that occurred in my family, will show you how easy it is to fall into old patterns of response.

One night I came in the back door, late and tired, to find a bag of trash torn open all over the back porch. Nate was in the kitchen putting the finishing touches on dinner. "There's trash all over the back porch!" I said in a tired, tense voice. I suspected our dog had torn open the trash bag that was waiting to be taken to the bin. I took the kitchen trash can to the porch, put the trash in it, and joined the family, by now at the dinner table.

Nate was angry. "How could you come in the house yelling at me like that? We were having a pleasant evening until you came in. The tone in your voice is mean. You need to take responsibility for how you make me feel."

I tried to declare my innocence with calm. "I just saw the garbage on the porch, made a statement about it, and cleaned it up. I don't see what was wrong with that."

"Your tone is mean and biting. It is unpleasant. It upsets me. I didn't have anything to do with the trash, and you came in acting mean."

I knew I was right about this one, and I did not think it would take long to demonstrate that. "I am not responsible for your being upset. All I said was that there was garbage all over the back porch."

Jon got into the fray. "Yeah. Your tone of voice makes me mad, too. You shouldn't talk in a way that is upsetting to us."

"I think you both have the same problem. Neither of you tolerate me getting upset or angry. I have a right to be upset and say it when I feel it." I knew my rights! I had spent the past eight hours encouraging people to speak their feelings. Our conversation was repeated in various forms without either side budging or understanding the other.

I finished dinner and went to lead a group therapy meeting. As I was sitting in the group, a lightbulb went off. I had blown the conversation by not listening reflectively to Nate and Jon! It did not matter whether I was right or not in the end. What they needed was to be heard. I told the group about the incident because it was such a good example of how I had justified myself instead of attending to the real problem. Of course, many were sympathetic to my right to express myself, but they wanted to know how I planned to clear up the conversation with Nate. I told them I would try reflective listening.

When I returned home, I said to Nate, "When I came home upset tonight about the garbage, my tone really bothered you, didn't it?"

"Well, I didn't know what you were talking about, but I thought you were accusing me of making a mess on the porch."

"I didn't mean to imply that you did anything wrong, and I'm sorry you felt accused."

"You just don't know the effect you have on us. Jonny feels it, too."

"You'd like me to understand that you feel accused, perhaps, whenever I'm angry. You think I'm saying you have been bad?"

By this time we were more sympathetic toward each other. I could appreciate how he had reacted to my coming in, irritated. He spoke without rancor. We did not make any "I'll never do that again" agreements, and I do not know who changed. But the theme of how mean I am has not been repeated in the year since this conversation.

The mechanics of reflective listening are easy, but getting yourself to do it instead of making the all-too-natural response of self-justification is

another matter. Many couples who come to me in therapy are on the verge of separating, but they leave the session feeling hope after one of them listened. They were not listening at home because as soon as one of them brought up a painful issue, it triggered an argument. Practice reflective listening when your partner is sharing experiences that do not involve feelings about you. After you have developed the habit of reflective listening, you will be able to do it when you are feeling more emotionally challenged.

If it happens often that one of you cannot listen, it may mean a lot of conflict has gone unresolved. If you do not get issues cleared up within a few months after you begin to apply the skills presented here, seek counseling.

DISCUSSION 5. *What can motivate you to use reflective listening when your spouse is expressing an opinion or feeling different from yours?*

For Practice

Schedule a date with your spouse this week, without your children. You might take a walk or eat out. Designate one person to speak and the other to listen reflectively. Suggestions for subjects to speak about are what you see, hear, smell, or taste at the moment; news items in your community or nation; a global issue, such as how to educate the poor or end world hunger; or a vacation you would like to take some time in your life. Listen reflectively to the first speaker until he or she has completed that topic. At that time, the speaker can become the listener. Continue doing this until you have covered several topics.

NOTES

1. Carl Rogers, *Client-Centered Therapy* (Boston: Houghton Mifflin Co., 1951).
2. Thomas Gordon, *Parent Effectiveness Training* (New York: Peter H. Wyden, 1970).

Chapter Seven

Positive Messages Create Love

In this chapter you will learn how to enhance the warmth and good-will in your relationship by appreciating, affirming, and praising your spouse. Those of you who naturally appreciate people will increase your ability to do that. Those of you for whom positive messages are uncharacteristic will be helped to incorporate these powerful communications into your behavior.

Positive Messages

Positive messages are the soul food that nourishes a marriage. They help couples get through difficult times. They create joy in the good times. They motivate spouses to do what is pleasing to the other. Positive messages can make a marriage satisfying even when there are many other problems. If there are more positive messages than negative ones, couples are usually satisfied with their relationship. Most people know they should appreciate and praise their spouses, but forget to do so in everyday life. It is much more natural to complain or criticize when there is a problem than to mention that all is well. Positive messages make us feel loved. In the absence of positive messages, it is hard to believe it when your partner says "I love you."

There are three kinds of positive messages: appreciation, affirmation, and praise. In our culture, we tend to think of all positive communication as praise, and we neglect appreciation and affirmation. The important difference between appreciation, affirmation, and praise is that each is spoken from a different point of view.

Appreciation is an expression of pleasure from the speaker's point of view. The message is "I value (like, enjoy) what you did." Appreciation is easy to communicate and rewarding to receive. Appreciation is commonly used by many people, so it is familiar. Appreciation tells another person that his or her deed was noticed and it benefited the speaker. Appreciation can motivate a partner to repeat the behavior because most partners enjoy pleasing their spouse.

An *affirmation* is an expression of empathy and understanding from the receiver's point of view. The message is "You have used a lot of effort (courage, integrity, skill, talent, endurance, for example) in your actions." Affirmations validate a person's motives and efforts, and validation is an important building block of identity. They are a communication of empathy, similar to reflective listening: "I see your good intentions." Although affirmations are not commonly communicated between spouses, they can be a powerful demonstration of understanding and acceptance. Our identity flourishes in the presence of someone who is affirming. We bond with persons who recognize the best in us and can experience God's presence in the relationship.

Praise is the speaker's evaluation of the receiver's behavior. Praise means, "You performed well." Praise is valuable in a marriage if it is used appropriately. Praise is used appropriately when both spouses recognize that one is more experienced or skilled in an area, such as a mother's understanding of care for toddlers or a husband's knowledge about cars. Praise can acknowledge the receiving partner's accomplishment. Praise should be used only as long as one spouse is in an apprentice or learner role. The problem with praise is that it can be a subtle message of superiority because it implies the person doing the praising is a more qualified judge. If praise is the only positive message used, the partner receiving praise can feel uncomfortable because of the implication of inferiority. Appreciation and affirmations should be generously applied to soften the judgmental nature of praise.

Those of you who have a preference for Feeling (see chapter 3, Myers-Briggs personality types) will probably find that you give positive messages naturally. You also derive great pleasure from receiving them. Those of you who have a Thinking preference will have more difficulty because you are a natural critic of yourself and others. When someone says something nice to you, instead of receiving it graciously, you are likely to judge whether you agree with the message or not. For example, I had to learn to enjoy compliments about my appearance instead of offering my own critical opinion.

It is easier to give positive messages when you also receive them. Sometimes couples are in a self-defeating pattern wherein each hopes the other will give appreciation or affirmation while, at the same time, each refuses to give those messages. If this is your situation, do not wait for your partner to change. Take the power of change in your own hands and start the cycle of appreciation, affirmation, and praise. I am not suggesting you should lie about your feelings, but simply notice the ways your partner contributes something positive in your life. If you cannot think of anything, reread chapter 5 on appreciating differences.

Summaries and a comparison of the three kinds of positive messages are in table 7-1.

Table 7-1.
Appreciation, Affirmation, and Praise: A Comparison

Appreciation	Affirmation	Praise
Starts with, "I like . . ." or "I appreciate . . ." or "I am grateful . . . ."	Starts with, "You did . . ." or "You are . . . ," followed by the receiver's feelings and intentions.	Starts with "You did . . ." or "You are . . . ," followed by the giver's opinion.
Communicates the giver's good feelings about the receiver's behavior.	Communicates that the giver understands the receiver's intentions.	Communicates that the giver has critically evaluated and approves of the receiver's behavior.
Feels good to receive.	Feels good to receive.	May or may not feel good to receive, depending on circumstances.
Motivates the receiver to repeat the behavior, unless the receiver has a conflict about the behavior.	Motivates the receiver to feel close and intimate with the giver. Does not motivate the receiver to repeat the behavior.	May motivate the receiver to repeat the behavior. May increase the receiver's fear of criticism. Over a long time, may increase rebelliousness in the receiver.

Expressing Positive Messages

When you make distinctions in what you feel, you can communicate with precision and accuracy. Table 7–2 represents the feelings associated with appreciation, affirmations, and praise. Use the table to expand your repertoire of expression. You will use these expressions in discussions related to positive messages. Expressing just what you feel helps your spouse understand you better. To save space, all forms of the words have not been included. For example, "grateful" is included but "gratitude" is not. Use any form that expresses your experience.

Table 7–2. Positive Feelings

accepted	ecstatic	real
adventurous	enraptured	refreshed
affectionate	empowered	relaxed
affirmed	enjoy	relieved
agreeable	enthusiastic	respected
alive	enticed	responsible
alluring	esteemed	responsive
amazed	excited	safe
amused	exhilarated	satiated
appreciative	fascinated	satisfied
approved	forceful	seduced
aroused	fine	seductive
astonished	fortunate	sexy
assertive	full	silly
attentive	funny	sincere
attractive	gay	soft
aware	generous	soothed
awesome	genuine	spontaneous
beautiful	giving	smart
bold	good	smug
brave	grateful	stimulated
breathless	great	strong
bubbly	happy-go-lucky	successful
calm	healthy	sure
carefree	helpful	sweet
caring	hopeful	sympathetic
capable	important	tender
captivated	impressed	terrific
cheerful	intimate	thrilled
close	joyous	tickled
comfortable	like	tolerant
comforted	lively	tremendous
competitive	loving	trustful
complete	lucky	understood
confident	lustful	useful
considerate	open	valuable
content	overwhelmed	valued
cool	overjoyed	voluptuous
coy	patient	warm
cuddly	peaceful	whole
curious	perceptive	willing
daring	pleased	wishful
delighted	proud	wonderful
desirous	puzzled	worthy
desirable	quiet	
eager	ravishing	

Appreciation

What follows is an example of a husband appreciating his wife, who has been a waitress for eight years. Notice that he is expressing his own feelings here.

Appreciation (a husband's experience): Congratulations for that promotion! Honey, I am so glad that you got promoted to management. I am proud of you for taking that waitress job and turning it into a career. I appreciate all your help in supporting our family.

Appreciation is an expression of pleasure about another person's behavior from the *speaker's* point of view. It is a personal response, rather than an objective evaluation. Appreciation plays an important role in marriage, informing your partner what you enjoy about her or him or what you like. It feels good to know that your efforts were effective and enjoyed by your spouse. I recently told Nate: "Nate, I really like this soup. The spiciness is just right for me. I like the selection of vegetables. Especially, I like that you left out the seaweed. And I am grateful that you made it and had it ready when I came home from work." Here I am referring to my personal response to the soup rather than sounding like an expert evaluating his soup. Another example is, "Jon, I am really enjoying the tomatoes from your garden. They are so plump and sweet."

The simplest form of appreciation is "thank you." It is important to say this when your spouse does things for you, even if it is something he or she is "supposed to do." It conveys that you are not taking your spouse's actions for granted and that you notice and benefit from them. Some people believe they shouldn't have to thank their spouse, that he or she was fulfilling a responsibility. This belief is usually ineffective in a marriage. Most partners like to be thanked, even for fulfilling their responsibilities.

Appreciation should go beyond "thank you" and should communicate details about what you liked. Details communicate valuable information to your partner. Your partner can please you again, if he or she chooses to. Many times in marital therapy I hear, "I've been doing (fill in the blank) all these years because I thought you liked it," only to have the partner say, "I don't really like it." In this situation there has been incomplete communication through the years. In the soup example above, I conveyed to Nate just what I liked about the soup. He may want to know what I enjoyed the next time he makes soup.

When you give appreciation, it should be sincere, something you believe. It is not difficult for most people to notice what they like about their partner. But if you are the type of person who habitually sees the

cup as half empty, practice looking for things you like about your partner. Complaints are discussed in the next chapter, so do not complain
when you are giving appreciation.

Difficulty Appreciating

If positive messages are so great, why aren't people generous about
giving them? Many people allow criticisms, hurts, and resentments to
interfere with expressing appreciation. You will always be able to find
faults. If you wait for your spouse to correct them before you affirm him
or her, you will wait a long time and live in a joyless marriage. Start
appreciating now. Don't wait for your conflicts to be resolved. I am not
implying that you should ignore conflicts. Expressing complaints and
managing conflicts are necessary to clear up negative feelings. (How to
deal with negative feelings will be discussed in chapters 8 and 10.) Just
don't forget to express appreciation.

If you and your spouse have been in conflict for a long time, you may
have difficulty finding something you appreciate about each other. Your
perception has changed from looking for things about your partner you
like to seeing only the things you dislike. If you are feeling alienated,
push yourself to notice something about your spouse that contributes
positively to your life. Or consider your spouse's past behavior. After all,
you appreciated that behavior at one time enough to marry.

> Liz is married to Arnold, who does not initiate sex with her, and she fears
> there is something wrong with him emotionally. Liz feels severely rejected
> and hurt. She criticizes everything Arnold does and often blows up in rages.
> When I noted that she is not providing positive communication, she said
> she could not think of anything good about him. My observations, using
> information she gave me, were that he comes home every evening after
> spending his days at work supporting his wife and two children; he is a
> devoted father, assisting frequently with child care and household chores;
> he is kind and sociable; he has many friends; he does not spend money
> frivolously. But Liz did not accept my observations because she did not think
> I knew the *real* Arnold. Liz recognized that her perception of her husband
> was a problem only after a close friend of theirs—who knew Arnold well—
> told her how attractive and helpful he is. Only then did Liz consider looking
> for what she liked about him. As Liz became more appreciative, Arnold
> took an interest in sex.

If you have difficulty identifying something your partner has done
that you appreciate, it probably means you are so aware of conflict that

you cannot think of anything positive. You will learn how to handle conflicts in succeeding chapters of this book, so that may take care of the problem. You may, however, need to see a counselor to help you work on conflicts. It is important to recognize that the problem is probably with your perception of your partner rather than that your partner does nothing that deserves appreciation. You need help becoming aware of what to appreciate. Ask people who know both of you to help you identify how your partner contributes to your life. Recall what you appreciated about your partner before you were married or when you were newly married. Use those memories when completing Exercise 1 on page 118.

Receiving Appreciation

Appreciation can be expressed in a variety of ways. For example:

> I like it when you hold my hand when we are with other people.
> I feel attractive.
> I feel more confident when you stay near me at the company party.
> Thank you.
> I was delighted when you stood up to my mother.
> I felt hopeful when you listened to me.

Most people receive such expressions of appreciation happily. However, there is usually more to say than the opener. You can share more information and express feelings more fully in two ways.

First, when your spouse appreciates you, listen reflectively before you just say thank-you. Reflective listening invites further sharing of information and feelings. The following conversation is in response to the first example of expressions of appreciation listed above.

> *Partner 1, appreciating:* I like it when you hold my hand when we are with other people. I feel attractive.
> *Partner 2, reflective listening:* You enjoy that, huh?
> *Partner 1, completing the thought:* Well, yes. I feel like you acknowledge our relationship when we hold hands. I feel special.
> *Partner 2, pleased:* Well, good.

Another way to encourage more sharing is to ask open-ended questions. You are encouraging greater expression from the person giving the appreciation, not fishing for compliments. The following conversation could occur in response to the fourth expression of appreciation listed above.

Partner 1, appreciating: I felt hopeful when you listened to me.

Partner 2, open-ended question: What did you hope for?

Partner 1: We've been fighting a lot lately. When you listened, I hoped maybe we could get along better.

Partner 2, reflective listening: You'd like us to get along better. I guess I should listen some more?

Partner 1, sounding finished: I'd like that.

In a relationship that has a lot of conflict, however, one partner may even criticize the appreciation, saying "You don't act like you like . . ." or "If you really like the way I . . . , you'd be more affectionate." If your partner rebuffs your appreciation, he or she may be feeling conflicts in the situation you appreciated. You will learn about resolving differences in chapter 8. In the meantime, continue to express appreciation at other times and in other situations. It will benefit the relationship, even when your partner does not seem to receive it.

✔ **EXERCISE 1.**

    Husband appreciates wife. **Husband, express to your wife appreciation for something specific. Use table 7–2 on page 114, to help you identify your feelings. Wife, acknowledge what you have heard by using reflective listening or asking an open-ended question. Say thank-you, if it is appropriate.**

    Wife appreciates husband. **Wife, express to your husband feelings about something that was pleasing to you. Use table 7–2 to help you identify your feelings. Husband, acknowledge what you have heard by using reflective listening or asking an open-ended question. Say thank-you, if it is appropriate.**

DISCUSSION 1. *How does it feel to give appreciation? How did you feel when you were receiving appreciation? How do you think you will feel about repeating the activity that your spouse appreciates?*

Affirmations

What follows is an example of a husband affirming his wife. Notice that he is speaking about her efforts and accomplishments. He is not giving his own opinions, but is saying how the promotion might feel from *her* point of view. The situation is the same as that described on page 115.

> *Affirmation (acknowledging a wife's efforts):* Congratulations for that promotion! Honey, you have made a great career out of your waitress job. You started waiting tables at a small-town cafe, working long hours for little pay. You kept working hard and now you're in the finest restaurant in the city. It was difficult to learn all the details of elegant service, but you stuck with it. You have even made friends with the people you work with and the regular customers. Your employers recognize how responsible you are. Now you've gotten promoted to management and you're going to make a lot more money!

Affirmations begin with "I affirm you for . . . ," or "I recognize that you . . . ," or "I notice that you . . . ," or you may simply describe your spouse's behavior and intentions. Your message should include details about the effort your spouse extended. In the example above, the husband simply described his wife's experience, from *her* point of view. He described in detail her hard work, which was rewarded by the promotion.

When you are giving an affirmation, it is not effective to point out your different point of view. In the example above, the husband could have had a different opinion. He could have thought she should have gone to college or gotten a professional job instead of waiting tables. If he had stated his point of view, his wife would not have felt his empathy or understanding.

An affirmation is acknowledgment that the person had good intentions, *from their own point of view*, not yours. In other words, affirmations are empathy. Affirmations validate a person, an important building block of identity. Affirming someone is a way to touch the soul, or the essence, of another human being. I believe that intentions reflect a person as God sees that person. Affirmations are soothing ointment that heals wounds. Your spouse's behavior may not have been effective, in the long run, but the intention was positive. Even someone's behavior that looks destructive can have a positive intention if you open yourself to understanding the person.

Affirmations make change and growth much easier because they make it unnecessary to protect our pride. When we are confronted with a fault, we want to say, "I'm fine the way I am. Don't expect me to change!" Sometimes we see trying to change or do something new as an admission of failure in the past. We get defensive. Being affirmed supports past behavior so that we can more easily try on something new. An affirmation says, "I acknowledge what a well-intentioned person you are." With that, ego can let go of its puny excuses and precautions, and step out of the shadows to risk a change. Affirmations motivate us to go beyond the constraints of what is known and comfortable. They release our energy and creativity.

Affirmations are not easy to make because they require empathy, that is, putting yourself in your spouse's place and experiencing the world as he or she would. When you affirm someone, it does not mean that you agree with or like the behavior. In fact, you may not like the behavior. You will need to set aside your own opinion or feeling in order to acknowledge your partner, which is not a natural act. It requires effort and practice to set ourselves aside to fully engage in another person's experience, which is inevitably different from our own. You experience some of this setting aside of self when you listen reflectively.

Persons with a Feeling preference feel empathy naturally and grasp affirmations easily. Persons with Thinking preference will be more challenged because they want to be "right," which is to promote their own point of view. However, empathy can be learned and practiced. If you are having particular difficulty with the concept of affirmations, you may be having difficulty setting aside your own point of view.

When I affirmed Nate for his parenting of Jon, our relationship changed for the better. During the first two years of our marriage Nate and I had heated arguments about our differences in parenting. I believed that he was too permissive with Jon and, as a result, Jon had little self-discipline. Jon did not accept discipline from me. Nate would argue just as vehemently that I was too stern, demanding, and unsympathetic to Jon. I believed all along that there were many things that Nate did to be a good father, but I had not told Nate.

Finally, one day I said, "Nate, I acknowledge that you put your heart and soul into being Jonathan's father after your divorce. You stopped working for a consulting company and became independently employed so that you could be available for him. You reduced your out-of-town consulting. You gave him just about everything he asked for. You opened your home for other children in the neighborhood to gather. You encouraged him to learn to play baseball and hockey by buying equipment and taking him to lessons."

This opened the door for Nate to tell me how difficult it was to care for a young son while he worked. He told me incidents of Jonny being locked out of his house all afternoon when he lost his key, and about the frustration of finding child-care workers to stay with him. I listened reflectively to Nate as he told me how guilty and anxious he felt about parenting. After this conversation, Nate felt that I understood him and he no longer had to argue with me. I could sense there was a change in him by his softer tone. In fact, he acknowledged my concerns about discipline.

I could have said that Nate spoiled Jonathan. I could have focused on the insecurity I feel from time to time because Nate is self-employed. But when you affirm someone, you do not say critical things. It is not the purpose of affirmations to focus on your issues. The purpose is to focus on your partner's positive intention, how your spouse is trying to work things out in the best way, regardless of the results.

Affirmations can refer to current efforts or to experiences growing up. Most of us had troubles in childhood that we had to overcome in order to be adults with character. All those troubles had their payoff in lessons learned and internal resources gained. If everything were given to us with no frustration as children, we would be unable to handle a world of frustration as adults. Those of us who did not have a troubled childhood had to learn to cope with a harsh adult world that we entered like tender shoots, soon trampled by tougher adults. So no matter what our background, all of us have suffered to become who we are. It is confirming and comforting for our partner to recognize the effort we expended.

We are much more likely to affirm our children than our spouse. Parents are often able to see that a young child's imperfect efforts are admirable within the context of normal development. For example, a parent may say, "You worked very hard on this picture! You used pretty colors and shapes. What is it?" as he or she attaches a colorful abstract drawing to the refrigerator with magnets. A parent will encourage a child learning to skate or ride a bicycle, even though the child may be struggling not to fall. When Jon ran track in seventh grade, he was, by far, the smallest child on the team. I wept with pride to watch him run as hard as he could and finish last. It would help our marriages if we were as understanding of our spouse's development.

Mike and Beth are an extreme example of the power of affirmations. Mike brought Beth to therapy because she was avoiding conversations and activities with her family and was always angry or unhappy. Both Mike and Beth thought all the problems were Beth's fault. She had had a difficult battle with breast cancer fourteen years earlier, when her children were young; she had a double mastectomy and felt unattractive. Mike was a successful stockbroker and had also been very involved in the care of the family. Typical of people with a Thinking preference, Mike was critical. Beth was equally strong in Feeling preference and desperately needed to hear something positive. As Mike saw it, he supported the family financially and also provided a lot of the daily care of the children, including meals. He acknowledged that he was completely unable to think of anything to appreciate or praise about his wife, a statement that caused so much pain she was unable to continue our session and left.

I pointed out that each of them had a problem. The problem was not that there was nothing good to say about Beth. The problems were that (1) Mike was unable to recognize and acknowledge Beth's strengths, and (2) Beth was so hurt that she withdrew instead of standing up for herself. Mike had difficulty understanding how to put himself in Beth's place in order to affirm her, and needed help in therapy to learn that. After many weeks, Mike learned how to make affirmations, how to put himself into his wife's experience. It was not easy for him, but here is what he finally told her.

Beth, when you had cancer, you must have been very frightened. You endured several hospitalizations. You had three small children whom you could not look after because you felt sick from the chemotherapy. It took great courage to live through that.

You have felt alone for the past fourteen years because I have not been loving with you. I have taken care of us and kept us going, but I have not been a loving companion. In spite of this, you still come to touch me and put your arms around me. Often, I rejected you. Yet you had the strength to keep reaching out to me.

Beth was moved by Mike's recognition of what she was going through and his affirmation of her efforts. In the following weeks she began interacting with people more, paying more attention to her appearance, calling friends, and talking with Mike and their children. Beth had stored a lot of anger toward Mike for his inability to affirm her, which she expressed in therapy. Beth gained courage to bring up things that had been bothering her, such as money, which Mike tightly controlled. Together, they learned to make joint decisions, including where to go away alone for a holiday.

Receiving Affirmation

Affirmations should be easier for you to learn than they were for Mike. It is an extreme case when one spouse is completely unable to affirm another. Couples participating in Recreating Marriage usually have more positive experiences to remember than Mike and Beth had. Here are other examples of affirmations:

That was a bold move, asking your boss for a raise.

It was difficult for you to grow up with parents who did not express affection.

You are pleased that the Marines respect your leadership.

You feel responsible for helping your brother overcome alcoholism.

An affirmation can be initiated by either the giver or the receiver. If you initiate ways to affirm your spouse, you enhance your spouse's feeling of being understood. If you are in need of affirmation, you can ask for that, reassuring yourself that your spouse empathizes with you. You can ask for an affirmation simply by saying "I need an affirmation" or "I've worked so hard (painting, cleaning, cooking, at my job) and I'm tired and cranky. Please affirm me for my hard work." This may be a good time to ask for a hug, as well. With practice, affirmations will seem more natural and your relationship will be more cooperative and feel more loving.

We appreciate and enjoy affirmations because they communicate that our spouse understands our point of view. You can receive the affirmation by saying thank-you or "I hear you," indicating you received the empathy. Often, an affirmation releases a flood of feelings and thoughts in the partner receiving it. The partner may respond by going into detail about the situation, after realizing that he or she is understood, as Nate did after I affirmed his effort to be a good father.

Sometimes, the receiver may not feel understood and may need to clarify his or her feelings. If this happens, listen reflectively to the clarification and then continue with the affirmation. For example, after Mike affirmed her, Beth might have said, "I didn't feel any courage. I did the only thing I could do." Her husband could reflect her feelings by saying, "You did not think of yourself as courageous. You were just surviving in the only way you knew." And then continue with the affirmation, "Still, you kept reaching out to me."

✔ **EXERCISE 2.**

Husband affirms wife. **Ask your wife what she wants to be affirmed for.**

Wife, consider asking for affirmation for effort put into any aspect of your life, not necessarily for positive results. Ask for affirmation about your growth and development from your difficult and troublesome experiences as well as for your successes. You can go back to early childhood experiences or more recent times. You can choose to be affirmed for surviving an upsetting experience or having overcome a personal obstacle, such as quitting smoking or

working hard to get your blood pressure down. You may want affirmation for caring for your children or for a spouse's parent.

Husband, begin your affirmations with one of the following: "I affirm you for . . . ," "I recognize that you . . . ," "I acknowledge that you . . ." or "I notice that you. . . ." Include details about the effort your wife extended.

Wife, don't forget to acknowledge that you received the affirmation.

Wife affirms husband. Reversing roles, wife, ask your husband what he wants to be affirmed for.

Husband, consider asking for affirmation for effort put into any aspect of your life, not necessarily for positive results.

Wife, begin your affirmations with one of the following: "I affirm you for . . . ," "I recognize that you . . . ," "I acknowledge that you . . . ," or "I notice that you. . . ." Include details about the effort your husband extended.

Husband, acknowledge that you received the affirmation.

DISCUSSION 2. *How does it feel to be the giver of an affirmation? How does it feel to be the receiver of an affirmation?*

Praise and Compliments

In the example that follows, the same husband who earlier affirmed and appreciated his wife is now praising her. Notice that the husband is assessing the value and effectiveness of his wife's choices.

Praise (a husband's evaluation): Congratulations on that promotion. Honey, you have done really well, getting promoted. You're very responsible to have started as a waitress in a small restaurant and now to move up to management in an elegant and expensive restaurant. I think you made a smart choice to work for a good company with a lot of opportunity.

Praise is an evaluation from the *speaker's* point of view. Praise and compliments are the same, and have a similar effect on a person. Examples of praise frequently given by spouses are the following: "That was a great dinner." "You handled the kids really well tonight." "The garden looks great. You did a good job." "That brown suit looks great on you." Praise can feel good if it is balanced with affirmation and appreciation. But praise is also closely related to criticism because both imply an evaluation of worthiness. Praise may seem patronizing if the receiver feels belittled by the evaluation. For example, if Nate tells me my driving has improved when I did not think there was any problem with my driving in the first place, I feel uncomfortable.

I am not suggesting that you avoid praising your partner, but that you use praise appropriately. Use it when you are really evaluating and judging your spouse and your judgment is wanted. Your husband *may* want your judgment about how he looks. Your wife *may* want your judgment about how she planned the stock portfolio. However, most couples do not use enough appreciation and affirmation, so give more of these.

Praise and criticism may work in circumstances where a clear authority or master provides feedback to a student or less-experienced person about performance. If you are learning a skill, it is useful to have critical feedback in order to know how to improve. But unless there is an unusual circumstance in a marriage, such as one spouse being a master and the other a learner, this kind of marital relationship is frequently unsuccessful. As soon as the learner begins to develop skill, he or she often becomes resentful about the well-meaning evaluations and the subordinate relationship. Anyone who has tried to teach a spouse to drive a car has had this experience!

Remember my appreciative remarks about Nate's soup? If I were to praise Nate about his soup, rather than appreciate it, I might say, "Nate, the soup you made is really good. You put the right amount of seasonings in. Not too much hot sauce. Your selection of vegetables is improved. You left out the unusual foods like seaweed, which has given soup an unpleasant texture in the past. You had dinner made on time for me when I returned from work." Notice the difference in this example of praising Nate's soup and the earlier example of appreciating it. Here, when I praise, I sound as though I am an authority, superior to Nate in knowledge about soup making. Perhaps I *am* an authority about soup and Nate is grateful for the feedback, but if I approach all my positive communication as though I am an authority, Nate is going to feel belittled.

Turning Praise into Affirmation and Appreciation

The pattern of superior and subordinate can be changed if the person who praises will add *affirmations* and *appreciation*, which imply equality in the relationship. Praise can be turned into appreciation simply by changing the message from a "You did . . ." to "I liked. . . ." Instead of saying, "You handled the kids really well tonight," you could say, "I liked the way you handled the kids tonight." This will probably inspire the question, "What did you like?" and you can express in detail what you appreciated. Here are some examples of praise turned into appreciation.

Praise: That coat is beautiful on you.
Appreciation: I like the way that coat looks on you. It's beautiful.

Praise: You are such a good coach. Those kids work hard for you and they respect you too.
Appreciation: I am impressed with the way you coach those kids. They work hard for you and they respect you too.

Praise: You are doing great with Peter. You were patient when he had his temper tantrum and you got him to bed on time.
Appreciation: I am relieved to see how patient you are with Peter, especially when he had his temper tantrum. You even got him to bed on time.

Praise: You are managing the budget really well. We have not overspent in two months.
Appreciation: Thank you so much for managing the budget. We have not overspent in two months.

Receiving Praise

Praise is often received and enjoyed by spouses who then spontaneously say thanks. If you are being praised for something complicated, such as a dinner party or a vacation, ask for more details so that you know what your partner is praising. If you or your partner feel uncomfortable receiving praise, turn the praise into appreciation.

If you have difficulty accepting any positive messages, you may not feel worthy of them. This is really a problem with feeling unlovable. Review chapter 1, "The Gift of Love," and begin to develop a belief that you are lovable.

✔ **EXERCISE 3.**
   Praise your partner for five things he or she did, of which you approve. Praise usually starts with a "You are . . ." or "You did. . . ." Include details about what your spouse did. For example, "Nate, you are a good stepfather to Ariana. You are generous with financial support and you spend a lot of time listening to her problems."

DISCUSSION 3. *How did it feel to give praise? How did you feel when you received praise?*

✔ **EXERCISE 4.**
   **Turn your praise in Exercise 3 into appreciation. Here is the exam-
   ple above turned into appreciation: "Nate, I like how you are being
   a stepfather to Ariana. I appreciate your generosity with money
   and that you spend a lot of time listening to her problems." Do you
   notice a difference between how you feel giving and receiving
   appreciation and praise?**

Positive Messages Motivate People

When you share your pleasure about something your spouse has
done, he or she is more likely to repeat the behavior than if you ignore the
behavior or express negative feelings. If your husband makes breakfast
and you tell him you enjoy it, you are positively motivating him. I am
grateful when Nate takes charge of the kitchen and I express my appreciation to him often for this. Motivating people positively produces good
feelings in people *without* dominating them.

The motivation works, however, only if your partner does not have a
conflict with the activity you like. Appreciation and praise will not motivate people who are confident in their identity and values to do something that they oppose. When your partner is opposed to a particular
activity, use requests and promises (see chapters 8 and 9) rather than
appreciation or praise as motivation.

Affirmations motivate people differently than do appreciation and
praise. Affirmations communicate that the speaker understands the
receiver. Feeling understood increases cooperation and goodwill in the
relationship in general. Since affirmations do not indicate what the speaker feels, they will not motivate the receiver to increase or decrease a particular behavior.

Some people believe it should not be necessary to express appreciation
for something a spouse should be doing anyway. This belief produces
ideas like, "My spouse should carry out responsibilities without needing
a pat on the back for everything." People who believe this deprive their
partners of the good feelings created by positive messages. Like weeds
crowding out the flowerbed, withholding appreciation allows negative
feelings of resentment and discouragement to crowd out goodwill. This
belief may be effective in dealing with some very independent souls who

don't need positive words, but it does not work with most partners. For most people, appreciation sweetens the experience of carrying out the tasks of life.

Control

Approval (appreciation and praise) can be used by one spouse to control the other: one partner can express appreciation, praise, love, affection, and sexual interest when things are going his or her way, and withhold all positive communication, including affection and sex, when displeased. This is the "silent treatment." Withholding positive contact is not an effective way to settle conflicts or get your way. Your spouse will feel hurt and dominated and may ultimately do what you want, but both of you will feel resentment. Over the years, these small, unresolved resentments grow into a brick wall.

Rather than staying silent when you are displeased with your spouse's behavior, express your negative feelings and work on the conflict that needs to be resolved. You will need to gain confidence that you can bring up conflicts successfully (see chapter 10). Changing a pattern of withholding positive communication is very difficult and takes a lot of effort, and you may need some professional counseling to break the pattern.

Dependency

People who are not confident about their identity and values may be strongly motivated by messages of approval. Many people like being praised so much that they will work hard to receive it, whether or not the activity being praised is beneficial to the person doing it. This pattern has been called "co-dependency" by some authorities. When someone continuously seeks approval, that person loses awareness of what he or she feels and thinks. Anger and bitterness can arise over time, not because the praising partner has been an ogre, but because the person who seeks to please loses his or her identity.

Often, though not always, it is women who come to therapy, unhappy that they have put so much time and effort into doing what their husbands want. They do not know what kind of life they want for themselves. The husband in this situation is accustomed to having his wife provide for him, and a change in her behavior is difficult for him to understand. When his wife becomes less responsive to his needs, he sees her as unloving. After all, he tells her often what a great job she is doing. What more could she want? Both are trapped in a pattern of the wife's seeking praise and approval, and the husband's need for his wife to please him. A marriage can get very rocky at this point and, indeed, some end in divorce. Approval seeking and the eventual loss of identity are intolerable in the long run. It requires patience and commitment on the part of both spouses to endure the changes while one partner develops an independent identity and the other learns to let go of the wish to *be* pleased.

DISCUSSION 4. *Think about a time when your spouse expressed appreciation or praise. Tell your spouse about the situation. How has your partner's appreciation motivated you?*

✔ **EXERCISE 5.**
Identify a behavior of your partner's that you like. Give your partner appreciation, affirmation, and praise about that behavior. In the example here, Nate had taken Jon and his friends on a wilderness camping and canoe trip. Follow the style here if you need to:

Appreciation: Nate, I'm very grateful that you took charge of the camping trip. You supervised Jon to get all the equipment and food packed. You met with his friends to be sure they were bringing what they should. Thank you for doing it all without me.

Affirmation: Nate, you worked hard to be sure this camping trip was successful. Spending a lot of time planning and packing was not easy or fun for you. Going camping with Jon and his friends in the wilderness shows how much you love him.

Praise: You did a thorough job planning and preparing for the camping trip with Jon. You supervised Jon to get all the equipment and food packed. You met with his friends to be sure they were bringing what they should. You are such a loving dad.

A Positive Attitude

Being able to recognize and appreciate good things in life creates health and energy and makes you pleasant company. A positive attitude means having thoughts of appreciation, affirmation, and praise about many things. Recognizing the good parts of life and expressing your feelings about them to your spouse benefits you and those around you and helps to combat discouragement, tension, and stress.

You can develop a habit of noticing good things by thinking, meditating, and praying about them. Some people may recognize these thoughts as praising God for blessings. Use the following examples of positive prayers to God, or you can write your own:

Appreciation: Dear God, I am grateful for this day and all its opportunities.

Affirmation: Oh, God, you have loved me even when I did not know you.

Praise: The pear tree in the backyard is beautiful this spring, God.

I am not suggesting that you avoid conflicts and problems. It is equally important to notice and solve problems. However, a positive attitude can give you energy to solve conflicts rather than turn away in fear.

✔ **EXERCISE 6.**
In your journal write to God three statements each of appreciation, affirmation, and praise.

For Practice

Give your spouse an expression of appreciation, affirmation, and praise daily for the next week.

Chapter Eight

Requests Create Action

Spouses usually tell their partners about something that is bothering them by accusing or complaining. This can produce a defensive response in the other partner and result in an argument. Making a request makes your desires known before an argument or accusation can begin. The purpose of this chapter is to show couples how to convey the power of requests clearly so that these requests become an irresistible replacement for accusations and complaints.

Requests and Promises Create Partnership

When a man and woman share their lives, one aspect of the partnership is determining what each will do for the other. Requests are a means to develop the kind of partnership that takes into account each other's needs, wants, and desires. The alternative is for each person to have unshared expectations and disappointments.

A request lets you start a conversation by telling your partner what you want. Thus, requests are half of the communication necessary to create a partnership. A request invites either a promise to do what you want or a refusal. The other half of the partnership communication is a promise, covered in the next chapter. Your partner will respond more positively to your request than to your anger, misery, and disappointment. However, requests are not a panacea. Just because you make a clear and reasonable (from your point of view) request does not mean your partner will do what you want. Your partner will usually do as you ask unless your request is in conflict with something your partner values. When the request presents a conflict for your partner, you will need to go through a process in which you brainstorm solutions together and find a way to satisfy both of you.

What can you depend on your spouse to do? Usually our behavior in marriage develops in response to expectations we learned from our families growing up, based on observations of how our parents treated each other and how we experienced our parents treating us. Often, without being aware of it, we expect our spouse to conform to what we learned or experienced in our family of origin. Because each partner has grown up with a different experience, the partners' expectations are often in conflict. And our own lives seldom duplicate our parents', so what worked for them may not work for another generation and in another social context.

Requests clarify expectations and are an important step toward strengthening a partnership. Clarifying expectations is especially important when children enter the family and their care requires a reorganization of labor. Our culture is in transition about the division of labor in childrearing. Many people can remember when most wives stayed at home to take care of children. Now some men stay at home while their wives work. More often, both parents work and wives hope husbands will be an equal partner in childrearing, home maintenance, food preparation, and care of clothing. The partners get confused about what each will do, and there may actually be too much work for both. Much argument, and even divorce, occurs because of uncommunicated expectations and the inability to resolve this conflict in roles. Expectations change when children grow up and leave home, and the marriage must change again. Spouses' focus turns from childrearing to desire for companionship in a partner. Also, spouses change and different things become important as a result of maturation and life experiences. A value that is fulfilling in one stage of life, such as achievement, may be replaced by another, perhaps friendship, later on. All these transitions hold potential for bumps in the marital journey.

Spouses participate in each others' lives in myriad ways. No matter what lifestyle you work out together, you are married because you want to be together in some form. Some husbands and wives are independent, each with their own careers, friends, cars, and hobbies. They may even work in different cities. They may need to schedule special time and activities to spend with each other. Another couple may spend much of their free time together, whether one or both work. They may share chores or sharply divide them. Making requests is one way of working out responsibilities and use of time in any lifestyle to the satisfaction of both.

Complaints

People generally deal with dissatisfaction in one of two ways: by complaining or suffering in silence. It is natural to complain when we do not like something. Complaints are the usual way we express what we want. In infancy, when we cry, we get fed. Children complain that they did not get as many cookies as their siblings, and the injustice is corrected. Adolescents complain that their peers have a much later curfew than they, and parents yield. By the time we create our own families, the habit of complaining is ingrained: "You are late again from work." "This place is a mess." "You don't give me enough affection." "The kids fight all the time." "You stay up too late." "You spend too much money." Complaints go on and on and seldom create much change. You may notice that these statements give you an uncomfortable feeling in the pit of your stomach.

You can complain about yourself or someone else, depending on who you think is responsible for your problem. If you complain about yourself with self-critical remarks and thoughts, you will deprive yourself of self-confidence and creative problem-solving ability. Most of us do this from time to time when we face a frustrating problem. But if you complain about yourself frequently, you may feel depressed and even hopeless.

Complaining about somebody else is blaming. Blame places responsibility on another person for your feelings or problem. When you make someone else responsible for your feelings, you have no power except in trying to get the other person to change. It is frustrating to spend your energy on pushing someone else to change when your only real power is over your own behavior. People who have a habit of blaming others are angry because they have given away their power to control their own lives.

Taking responsibility for one's own experience is a difficult concept for some people. Some people have such a strong habit of blaming others that they never realize they can control their experience by behaving differently. It seems obvious to them that the other person caused their unhappiness. It is natural to feel anger, hurt, frustration, or sadness when you do not get something important to you. Often a person is stuck with the belief, "If you were different, I would be happy."

A more effective belief is, "I believe there is a solution to my problem. I request that you, my partner, help me develop a solution. If you are not available, I will use other resources, without any resentment." The belief that you are responsible for your experience is the most powerful way to produce effective and active problem solving. If you believe that your partner is causing your unhappiness—or is the source of your joy—you are a passive recipient rather than an active problem solver. You count on your partner to do what will make you happy, but your partner cannot make you happy. It is impossible for one person to make another happy. You must be the source of your feelings. (Managing your emotions is discussed in chapter 10.)

It is too much of a burden for your partner to be responsible for your happiness. Your spouse has trouble enough being responsible for his or her own happiness. If you develop your own ways to enjoy life, however, your partner may be liberated from your constant care and take pleasure in your company.

Some people, sometimes even without being aware of what they are doing, combine complaints, uttered on a grand scale, with intense expression of emotions, such as anger, hurt, helplessness, or sadness. The receiver of these emotions feels coerced and dominated. *Coercion* and *domination* (used interchangeably) refer to a more extreme use of negative emotions or the withholding of positive emotions to dominate others. The message in coercion is, "If you do not do as I ask, I will use my anger, upset, sadness, helplessness, or other negative feelings to make you feel bad." The thinking is, "If you want to avoid my anger, you will treat me the way I want to be treated."

Domination and coercion create a win-lose relationship. Domination creates a loss of identity in one person and is accompanied by resentment or, even worse, feelings of deadness inside. To a person who is being dominated by another person, life feels meaningless. This person has little spontaneous expression, and his or her life feels as though it belongs to someone else. Feeling dominated may cause severe depression or physical pain. The dominated person may contemplate leaving or be vulnerable to having an affair. The dominating spouse may not be an ogre but may be applying communication methods learned from childhood that are ineffective in marriage. Anyone who is participating in a coercive relationship should get professional help.

Some people decide not to complain but instead to suffer in silence. These people learned in childhood that complaints were destructive and unproductive. Perhaps a parent was a chronic complainer (a "world class" complainer, as a client described his father) or complaints escalated into angry and frightening arguments. The silent method of dealing with differences is not effective either. Silent complaints (those you think about but do not express directly) produce ulcers, headaches, fatigue, and other physical ailments, as well as depression. When the silent sufferer cannot endure the situation any longer, that person may leave the marriage. The breakup often is shocking because the spouse is not aware of the partner's dissatisfaction.

DISCUSSION 1. *How did your parents communicate their wants to each other? What was the result of their communication?*

DISCUSSION 2. *Do you and your spouse use complaints? How do complaints affect your marriage? Does either of you suffer in silence?*

Requests

You can avoid these uncomfortable emotions and unpleasant experiences if you learn to make requests. *Requests* are statements of the speaker's desire for something from the listener. Requests identify an issue and present a compelling invitation for a response of either acceptance or refusal.

Most people start requests with "Could you . . . ?" "Would you . . . ?" "Please . . ." or "I want you to . . .":

> "Could you stay with the baby so I can go shopping?"
> "Would you cut the grass?"
> "Please put gas in the car."
> "I want you to make dinner."

This way of communicating works well some of the time. As long as you and your partner are getting along, do what comes naturally. But if your partner does not respond to your usual type of request, be more direct by saying, "I request that you. . . ." This specific wording usually compels the other person to think through the request and provide a response by accepting or declining the request. It is more productive than the other forms of making requests because it makes the other person *decide* what he or she will do. You may feel awkward at first saying "I request," but keep at it because these words will gain your spouse's cooperation in solving conflicts before they intensify.

When Nate and I married, I was a complainer and Nate suffered in silence. We remember being stuck. I complained that Nate worked too much and was out of town too often. Sometimes his work interfered with other commitments. I was overwhelmed with a new stepson and needed Nate to help bring order to our family. We were adding a bathroom to the house during the ice and snow of winter, and that created stress for me. My natural inclination was to bark at him, to communicate my misery. To add to my frustration, he tuned me out. Sometimes I felt unloved and avoided. Nate felt it was not safe to express his own experience. He thought he was strong enough to outlast whatever bothered him; it would go away eventually. Probably he hoped my complaining would go away. You can see that it is but a short step to hoping that *I* would go away! Luckily, during the first year of marriage Nate and I learned to make requests.

Requests can create peaceful transactions in a family and change family situations for the better.

Ilene, a client, came for therapy for depression because her family life was so unpleasant. She and Hal had been married for twenty-three years and had three teenagers at home. Hal was a yeller. When anything was not as he anticipated (which was often), he yelled. The children would get upset and usually yell back. Hal refused to join Ilene for therapy because he thought he was perfectly normal and everyone else was hopeless. Ilene caught on quickly to making requests and she taught her children to respond to Hal's anger by politely asking if he had a request. Whenever Hal requested something, they responded positively to his requests, because the requests were usually quite reasonable. If a person had an objection to a request, the family would offer other options. In a few weeks, Hal's yelling subsided, and the family felt relieved. Although Hal did not participate in counseling, the introduction of requests by his family changed him.

Note the difference between complaints and requests—and the responses to them—in the two examples that follow:

Example 1

Nate's Complaint: The dog is really dirty and smelly. You know I can't stand to have the dog in our bedroom when she is smelly.

My Response: There is no request to respond to. Of course, the displeasure is obvious, and I know if I want to make him happy I should wash the dog. I hear the implied criticism that I have delayed too long washing the dog, and I feel defensive. I might even argue about how busy I have been and point out that he could do it himself. My partner will not know whether I am committed to washing the dog at the end of the argument. I can delay and avoid.

Example 2

Nate's Request: I request that you wash the dog. When the dog is smelly, I notice it right away and it bothers me a lot. I feel invaded by the dog when my bedroom smells like a dog.

My Response: I am forced to decide whether I will or will not wash the dog, and to tell my partner my decision. It is difficult to argue with my partner's experience. The only thing I need to consider is whether or not I will wash the dog. In this case, I recognize my commitment to having my partner be comfortable with the dog. I agree to wash the dog by Sunday.

Requests are an effective means of engaging other people's participation in our lives. For instance, when Nate ran in a five-kilometer race, the first organized race in which he participated, he requested that I go to the event to support him. I accepted his request and met him at the water tables to cheer him on. If he had not made the request, I might have stayed home doing chores and he could have been disappointed, perhaps would even have felt rejected and angry.

You can educate your family to make requests instead of complaints. Even young children can learn to do this. A kindergarten teacher in Recreating Marriage taught her class to make requests. Now, when a child breaks in line, for example, instead of squabbling and hitting, the offended child will say, "You broke in line in front of me. I request that you go to the back of the line." And the line breaker does.

Uncomfortable Feelings Identify Requests

If you can, ask for what you want before any unpleasant feeling develops. If you have a habit of noticing what you want and asking for it, you are fortunate. However, most people complain rather than identify a need or a desire. Even if you know that you should make requests, sometimes you will not know what you want and will need help in sorting through your thoughts and feelings. You can get ideas about what you want by talking through thoughts and feelings with your partner.

Behind most complaints (your own or your partner's) you should be able to identify a request. The easiest way to recognize what you need is to notice what you complain about. When you complain, ask yourself, "What would satisfy this complaint?" For example, you may complain, "You aren't affectionate enough with me. You don't cuddle with me in front of the T.V. any more. You don't snuggle with me in bed." You can make the request, "I request that you be more affectionate with me and that we snuggle in front of the T.V. and cuddle in bed."

If you are feeling attacked or criticized, your partner probably has a complaint that needs to be changed into a request. You can help your spouse identify what she or he wants by using reflective listening and then asking, "Do you have a request?" This will give your spouse an opportunity to think through the want and to say it. Or your spouse may say, "No, I don't want anything. I just want to complain." In which case it is helpful to listen reflectively and to be sympathetic.

Sometimes we may not know enough about ourselves to know what we want. We may be confused and conflicted. Internal conflict—that is, a mixture of contradictory feelings—is common. This can be sorted out by talking with someone who can listen reflectively for a while to clarify the want. If your spouse is confused about what he or she wants, listen reflectively until the spouse asks for your opinion or makes a request. When spouses listen reflectively to help each other sort out conflicts, their marriage grows strong and satisfying.

In the example below, Donna is complaining to her husband, Lou, about their adult son, Larry, who did not send a card for her birthday. As Donna complains and Lou listens, she figures out what she wants. The conversation satisfies Donna's need for intimacy with Lou because he understood her, and she then got results by requesting help.

> *Donna [bristling]:* Larry did not send a card, let alone a present for my birthday. He did send an e-mail saying "happy birthday." That required no effort from him. I feel insignificant in his life. It really bothers me.
>
> *Lou [sympathetic, and expressing his own opinion]:* After I told him a week in advance about your birthday, it irritates me that he was negligent.
>
> *Donna [becoming even more upset]:* Larry told me in his e-mail that he forgot and that it was an honest mistake. Now I find out that he knew it was my birthday and lied to me. I am really angry with him.
>
> *Lou [recognizing that Donna needs to be heard and listening reflectively]:* You are mad about this. Not only did Larry neglect your birthday, but he lied as an excuse.
>
> *Donna:* I'm mad and I'm confused. I don't understand why he would lie when he knows he would get caught in it. I don't know what to say to Larry. I request that you call him and find out what is going on. Maybe by then I will calm down and be able to talk to him.
>
> *Lou:* Okay, I can do that.

> As she spoke, it occurred to Donna that she was confused about her son and wanted more information. She also wanted time to calm down. She asked Lou to help her by calling Larry.

Frequently, a spouse—a wife, for example—who is not familiar with reflective listening or undisciplined in using it will be unable or unwilling to do it. When her husband has a conflict, she may express her strong opinion about that conflict. This may inhibit him from exploring his conflict further. Worse, she may interrupt him before the conflict is fully expressed, to present her own point of view. This provides no help at all to her confused husband. In the following example, Denise, a high school teacher, is considering going to graduate school in psychology after her children leave home but is not sure whether she wants to spend so much time and effort in school at this time of her life. She begins to share her misgivings with her husband, Ray.

Situation 1

Denise [tentatively]: I think I would like being a psychologist more than teaching, but I don't know if I could be a full-time student again and do all that work. You know, I have been thinking a lot about seeing what it would take to go to grad school.

Ray [interrupts]: I thought we agreed you would work. We can't afford for you to stop working and go to school. We're still paying the kids' college loans.

Denise drops the subject, unable to sort out her thoughts with Ray and come to her own conclusion.

Situation 2

Ray should have listened reflectively and then replied: "Graduate school seems to be important to you, but you are worried about whether you want to do all the work that would be required."

If Ray had listened, Denise might have continued exploring the issues and eventually recognized that she wanted to make a request, such as, "I request that we make a budget that will allow me to go to school." Or she might have discovered she did not want to make all the changes necessary to be a student. If she just drops the conversation, as she did in Situation 1, she may live with a nagging sense of regret or become depressed.

When Denise finished her conversation, Ray then would have had his turn to talk about his financial concerns.

If your spouse does not know how to listen reflectively, request that he or she listen quietly to you as you talk about your conflict. Or talk with a friend or relative who can listen reflectively. Then you can return to your partner and make a clear request. If you cannot talk to anyone about your conflict, see a therapist to practice sharing your thoughts with someone.

DISCUSSION 3. *Think of a time when you were confused about what you wanted. What was your conflict? What were some of your feelings? Use table 8–1 to identify some of your feelings. Whom did you talk with about the conflict? What requests did you make when you became clear about what you wanted?*

Table 8–1. Uncomfortable Feelings

abandoned	crabby	furious	nasty	squelched
aching	cranky	greedy	nervous	smothered
accused	crazy	grief	numb	starved
agony	critical	grim	obsessed	stiff
alienated	criticized	grouchy	offended	stifled
aloof	crushed	grumpy	ornery	strangled
aggravated	cut down	guarded	out of control	stubborn
aggressive	deceived	guilty	overwhelmed	stunned
alone	deceptive	hard	panicky	stupid
angry	degraded	hassled	paralyzed	subdued
anguished	demeaned	hateful	peeved	submissive
annoyed	demoralized	helpless	perturbed	suffocated
anxious	dependent	hesitant	petrified	tainted
apart	depressed	hollow	phony	tense
apologetic	deprived	horrified	powerless	terrified
apprehensive	deserted	hostile	pressured	ticked
argumentative	despair	humiliated	pulled apart	tight
attacked	desperate	hung up	put down	timid
badgered	destroyed	hurt	quarrelsome	tired
baited	different	hyper	regretful	tormented
battered	dirty	ignorant	rejected	torn
beaten	disappointed	ignored	rejecting	tortured
belligerent	disconcerted	impatient	removed	trapped
belittled	disgraced	impotent	repulsed	tricked
bereaved	disgruntled	incompetent	repulsive	ugly
betrayed	disgusted	incomplete	resentful	uncertain
bitter	distant	insecure	resistant	uncomfortable
bored	distraught	insignificant	revengeful	unfriendly
bothered	distressed	insincere	rotten	unhappy
bound up	distrusted	insulted	ruined	unimportant
boxed in	distrustful	intolerant	sad	unimpressed
bristling	dominated	irate	scared	unstable
broken up	domineering	irked	scolded	upset
bruised	doomed	irresponsible	scorned	uptight
bugged	double-crossed	irritated	screwed	violent
burdened	down	jealous	self-centered	vulnerable
burned	dreadful	jittery	self-conscious	weak
burned up	edgy	left out	selfish	whipped
careless	elated	lonely	separated	wild
callous	embarrassed	lost	shattered	wiped out
cautious	empty	low	shocked	withdrawn
cheated	enraged	mad	shot down	worried
choked up	exasperated	malicious	shy	wounded
cold	exposed	mean	sickened	zapped
complacent	foolish	miserable	sinking	
conflicted	forced	misunderstood	sneaky	
confused	frightened	moody	sorry	
concerned	frustrated	mystified	spiteful	

✔ **EXERCISE 1.**

1. **In your journal write a list of five complaints about your life, your family, or your spouse. Use table 8–1 to identify what you are feeling.**

2. **Share your list with your spouse. Express the feelings you noted in your journal. Spouses should listen reflectively to the complaints, reflecting back the complaint so that the complainer feels heard.**

3. **When one spouse finishes, the other shares five complaints and receives reflective listening.**

4. **Tell your partner what you feel when you hear complaints.**

Beliefs Can Get in the Way of Making Requests

Beliefs are powerful motivators, but they can prevent us from functioning effectively. Beliefs that prevent effective functioning are "ineffective beliefs." Beliefs about making requests can inhibit a spouse from making requests. It is hard to recognize an ineffective belief, because the belief seems like a fact until its flaw is exposed. You will know you have an ineffective belief if you have trouble making requests. Many people have ineffective beliefs about requests. Here are some that many people hold.

Typical Ineffective Beliefs about Requests

1. If my partner loved me, he (or she) would do this without my having to ask for it.

2. I am not worthy of having my need met. I am not lovable enough.

3. I'll owe something in return.

4. If my partner wanted to do what I request, she would already be doing it. I may as well not ask.

5. If my partner says no, it must mean we are incompatible, so I don't want to test it and risk losing the relationship.

Effective Beliefs about Requests

You can, however, develop effective beliefs, such as the following:

1. My partner does not know what I need until I ask, and this unawareness of my needs is not an indication about my partner's love.

2. I am worthy of having my needs met. I am lovable.

3. I will give to others when I desire to give, not when I feel obligated.

4. If my partner is not already doing what I want, it may be for a variety of reasons, such as lack of awareness of what I want. A request may help me get a response.

5. If my partner says no, there may be another option that would work for both of us.

Changing ineffective beliefs requires self-examination and giving yourself the time to trust a new belief. If you have an ineffective belief about requests, the Discussion below may help change the way you think about them. Another way to change your belief about requests is to watch other people make requests and notice how effective they are.

DISCUSSION 4. *Can you think of some beliefs that can interfere with requests? Talk with your spouse about them.*

Requests with Sharing Motivate Others

By making requests we can have a powerful influence on getting what we want. The power comes from giving people a choice. Requests give someone the freedom to say yes or no. When people are given a choice, they are more cooperative and more likely to grant the request because they do not need to protect themselves from feeling dominated. For example, if Nate requests that I help make a budget, I have the freedom to choose. Unless I have a conflict with doing this, I will. But if he tells me that I *have to* make a budget with him in a demanding, threatening, or coercive way, I do not feel I have a choice and I do not feel respected.

Requests present an issue without blaming. The spouse is not at fault for not having already done it. For example, if Nate requests that I help make a budget, I do not have to hear how badly I have mismanaged the money, which would make me less willing to cooperate. When you respect your spouse's personhood, you foster cooperation. Your spouse is very likely to grant a request if the request does not conflict with his or her values.

You can make more effective requests by sharing. *Sharing* enriches your request with details, personal meaning, and information, and enables your partner to understand how important the request is to you. It is not intended to be a persuasive argument about why the request should be granted, which is likely to stimulate an equally persuasive objection. How would you respond to each of the requests below? The first example does not include sharing; the second does.

Request 1: Susan, I request that you keep the checkbook and balance the statements.

Request 2: Susan, I request that you handle the management of our money. I've been working long hours. I get bored with details. I get really confused about this computer checkbook and I am frustrated with it. You like being right on top of how much money we have, so you might be happier if you keep up with the checkbook and bank statements.

In the first request we hear what the person making the request wants, but do not have much sympathy for him. Susan might respond, "You're doing fine with it. No, I don't want to." In the request with sharing, we understand his thoughts and can appreciate his request. We know what the request means to him and how important it is. If we know something is really important, we are more likely to be motivated to provide it.

✔ **EXERCISE 2.**
   Wife, look at your list of complaints. Change one of your com-plaints into a request. Give your husband specific information about why the request is important to you. Husband, listen reflec-tively in order to receive the request clearly. Do not accept or decline the request.

   Then reverse roles: Husband, change one of your complaints into a request. Wife, use reflective listening.

   Taking turns, change all your complaints into requests.

DISCUSSION 5. *Tell your spouse what you feel when you receive a request. Tell your spouse what you feel when you make a request.*

Declining a Request

Many people try to avoid an answer by saying "maybe" or "I'll try" or "I'll see if I can." Another avoidance strategy is to accept the request and then not follow through. Clearly declining a request benefits the person making the request far more than indirect messages or responses because declining makes the issue clear. The person has no false hopes and no promises are broken.

A person can respond clearly and effectively in two ways to a request: accept it or decline it. Accepting the request means you will do it immediately or make a promise about doing it. (A promise confirms how the request will be carried out and when. I discuss this further in chapter 9.)

We should not, of course, expect the world to give us everything we want if only we ask. It is critical to your marital relationship that each of you be able to decline a request and say no, although it is normal to be disappointed when a request is not granted. When your request is declined, respect your partner's answer, and seek solutions together.

Spouses want to please each other. It is difficult to openly deny what your spouse wants. Often it is women who have difficulty saying no. Women have the double whammy of having more Feeling preference and being taught by their culture to be giving, helpful, and nurturing, to care for another's needs. However, men who have Feeling preference can also have difficulty declining requests.

Declining can be an unpleasant experience for both partners—the requester and the decliner. However, it is vital to be able to decline a request. If a person cannot say no, he or she ends up doing things that feel uncomfortable and eventually cause resentment or depression. Making a personal choice and saying no to some requests gives people the energy and vitality to say yes to other things. Ultimately, no one can love a partner who controls his or her life. The partner may not actually be diabolical and controlling, but it can feel that way for someone who lacks the power to choose.

Declining can be done without alienating your partner. When you decline your partner's request, communicate flexibility, compassion, and consideration so that he or she knows you took the request seriously. There are three ways to decline a request and still communicate flexibility and caring. Each makes the decline productive and demonstrates your interest in your spouse.

First, decline, and give a more acceptable offer. You can receive the request, using reflective listening (to make sure you heard accurately), and then provide an offer more acceptable to you.

Karen's request with sharing: Tom, I request that you go with me to visit my parents this Thanksgiving. It is very important for me to share my family with my parents. They are getting older, and I want to spend time with them while they are healthy and can enjoy it.

Tom's more acceptable offer: You would like me to go with you to visit your parents. I recognize how important your parents are to you. But spending five days in the country is not enjoyable to me. I suggest that I go to visit with you and the family once a year, and not go this Thanksgiving.

Second, decline, and offer help. You can receive the request, decline the request, but demonstrate concern and willingness to help your spouse solve the problem some other way.

Karen makes the same request with sharing in the example above; Tom declines the request with willingness to help: I do realize how important spending time with your parents is to you. (He reflects her point of view.) But I don't like to go to the country. I don't have anything to do to occupy my time. We just watch T.V., go fishing, or eat. No, I won't go. If you and the kids want to go, that would be okay with me. I could rearrange my schedule to take you to the airport. You would avoid the train ride and lugging your suitcases.

Third, decline, and brainstorm solutions. You receive the request, decline the request, and recognize a conflict of values. If your partner's need is not easily met, you are probably dealing with a conflict between you that is appropriately handled by negotiating. Negotiating a conflict is a process by which both people identify clearly what the issues are and brainstorm solutions. Then both people pick solutions that work for each person. Either partner can recognize a conflict in values if one of you becomes upset or cannot accept a spouse's response. In the example below, Tom declined Karen's request. This made Karen aware that she had not shared some information about why this trip was important to her. Karen could not accept Tom's answer because his solution conflicted with her values.

Karen makes the same request; Tom declines with another offer: I recognize how important it is for you to visit your parents. (He reflects her point of view.) But, I don't like to go to the country. I don't have anything to do to occupy my time. We just watch T.V., go fishing, or eat. I prefer not to go this time, and instead I'll go next summer. (He makes another offer.)

Karen states there is a conflict to negotiate: "It's difficult for you to sit around without activities that interest you. (She appreciates his point of view.) But this Thanksgiving is my parents' fiftieth wedding anniversary, and I want to celebrate that with them. Not only that, my aunt and uncle are celebrating their sixtieth anniversary, and the whole family is getting together.

It is very important to me that we go this Thanksgiving, and after that, if you come with us once a year, that would be okay with me.

Tom accepts Karen's invitation: This visit seems to be special. I will go with you this Thanksgiving. Is it really okay with you if I visit just once a year after this year?

Karen: That's fine.

Karen has revealed more information about what the request means to her, and indicates there could be a conflict between her and her husband about this if he continues to decline. If Karen and Tom did not have an obvious solution, they could continue to brainstorm options:

> Tom could create his own activities during the visit by taking along a laptop computer or books.
> Tom could plan visits with his in-laws to places of interest.
> Tom could take videotapes that would interest him.
> Tom could hike while other family members fish.

We would like all our requests to be granted, but because we live with a person who has a separate identity, some of our requests should be refused. Refusing requests provides people with freedom to respond wholeheartedly to another request.

When All Your Requests Are Declined

If you are sure your requests include sharing and your partner consistently declines all your requests, your partner may be refusing to participate in the relationship. Withdrawal from the relationship can be due to deep hurt or depression. In this case, consult a marital therapist. For example, if your partner has had a pattern of always accepting requests because he or she could not say no, there may be a swing to the opposite behavior of saying no to everything until the person gains confidence in his or her ability to decline.

Sometimes a partner (usually one with an Introvert preference) will buy time to think about a request by saying no before even considering the request. Saying no before saying yes is a matter of style, and the person may actually accept a request after thinking about it. Learning to decline requests that include sharing will help an introvert think through the reasons he or she is declining the request, which provides an opportunity for more satisfying solutions. Exercise 3 is intended to help you learn how to decline requests, so do not worry about whether the request is reasonable.

✔ **EXERCISE 3.**

Wife, select one of your requests to make of your husband. Share what the request means to you.

Husband, give three declining responses, for practice: (1) Decline the request with another offer. (2) Decline with interest and willingness to help. (3) Decline the request and brainstorm other solutions.

Then change roles. Husband, now make a request, following the instructions above. Wife, decline in the same three ways.

DISCUSSION 6. *How does it feel to hear your partner decline your request? How does it feel to receive no for an answer?*

For Practice

Each day during the next week, notice your partner's complaints and ask him or her to make a request. If your partner does not complain, ask your partner to make a request anyway. As you hear each request, accept or decline it.

Notice your own complaints. Change each complaint into a request.

Chapter Nine

Promises Create Trust

When someone makes a request and another person agrees to it, a promise is made. The purpose of this chapter is to strengthen the value of making and keeping promises, so that marriage partners can foster trust and security as well as independence and freedom in the marriage.

What Is a Promise?

Many people have not learned to keep promises. If you and your spouse are not careful about keeping promises, you are in good company. However, you can begin now to make promises that you are willing to keep and to develop strategies for keeping them. This will be a gradual learning process, so be patient.

We often use the word "promise" when an agreement is especially important and we have a strong intention to keep it. Promises, when kept, create trust. When I was a child, if another child broke a promise, it was considered shameful and disgraceful. In a marriage and family *all* agreements should be kept with the same intention that is paid to a "promise." Otherwise family members will not trust each other's word.

Wedding vows are the familiar promises that come to mind regarding marriage. We promise to love, honor, and care for each other until we die. What happens to this promise? Why are so many people unable to keep it? My clients who are divorcing did not make the promise lightly. I was unable to keep this promise in my first marriage. My husband and I did not keep it because we did not know how to make promises that were good for us and the marriage on a daily basis and keep them. We were thus unable to work out a satisfying partnership and our marriage broke up.

Requests and promises are partners. *Requests* give direction and motion to a relationship. *Promises* are the fulfillment of the request; they create trust. For example, your wife asks you to be home in time to take care of the children so that she can go to a meeting. You say you'll do it. This is a promise. Your husband asks you to stand up for him when your mother criticizes him. You agree to do it. This is a promise. A promise is a statement of intention to complete a specific action at a particular time.

Through making and keeping promises things get done and a partnership is created.

We enhance our capacity for relationships by identifying, making, and keeping appropriate promises. As we make promises, we learn to do what is necessary to keep them and so, in the process, we discover our limitations. When we overcome a limitation in order to keep a promise, we stretch or develop our abilities and grow.

To get me to commit to giving a dinner party to celebrate the birthday of a good friend, Nate promised to do most of the work. I told him all about my objections: The house looks shabby because of cracked plaster and peeling paint. The floors are dirty. I do not want to spend time preparing an elegant meal.

Nate made several promises that I trusted enough to agree to the dinner party with enthusiasm. He promised to plaster and paint the walls, to wash and wax the floors, and to shop for groceries and help with dinner. Nate had never plastered large cracks in walls. In addition, we had no matching paint for repainting after the plastering was completed. After making the promises he went to the hardware store to get supplies and information about how to repair the plaster. He took a chip of old paint to the paint store, which, by a miracle of modern technology, analyzed the color by computer and produced paint the exact color of the old paint, "Bender Blue" (dubbed by the paint store), with which he could touch up the repaired portions of the walls without having to paint the entire living room, dining room, and hall before the party. He bought wax remover and cleaned the floors, retrieved the old buffer from the basement, and shined them. And he shopped for groceries and helped with preparation.

Because Nate kept his promises, we could relax the day of the party and enjoy the bustle of family activities. The morning of the party we attended a business meeting; we had lunch with Dylan (who was visiting), and we spent the afternoon preparing food with an anticipation of pleasant company. The evening was so enjoyable that I wondered why we don't do this more often. And the house looked lovely even after the party. All of it was possible because Nate learned what he needed to know about plastering and painting, organized his time, and delivered on his promises. I must say on my behalf (or is it in my defense?) that I was heavily scheduled with clients during this time, while he had more time available.

DISCUSSION 1. *What does the word "promise" mean to you? Does it evoke any childhood memories?*

DISCUSSION 2. *Tell your spouse about a promise you made to him or her and kept. Why did you make the promise? Was the promise in response to a request?*

Freedom and Partnership

There is always tension in marriage between the freedom to live without being restrained by our partner and our commitment to that partner. Requests and promises are the tools by which we regulate both our own freedom to do what pleases us and honor the values of another person. Making requests and promises allows us to maintain some freedom to express our personal identity while nurturing a relationship.

The combination of freedom and commitment allows us to express our identity and live the life we choose. When we act alone we seem limited only by our own capabilities and resources. It can be exhilarating to live by one's own means without having to consider another person. One does not have to make joint decisions about such things as cars, children, where to live, what job to take, whether to go to the ball game or theater. Some people avoid marriage in order to sustain the freedom they want.

Developing a relationship with both freedom and partnership is not easy, but it is possible and extremely rewarding. You will have the opportunity for companionship with someone you know well and can count on. You have the joy of loving contact. You can participate in building a history together with common memories. And you have access to the talents and gifts that a partner might bring to your life. You have the opportunity for growth that is provided only by a partner holding up a mirror for you to see yourself, the feedback given by a loving spouse. What you don't have is the freedom to behave as you want *without* affecting another person. But, as you learn how to make requests and keep appropriate promises, your relationship will achieve more freedom and partnership.

DISCUSSION 3. *Think of a time in your life in which you felt the most freedom. What were you doing? How did you feel? Did your sense of freedom end? When and how did it end?*

Integrity: The Power of Keeping Your Promise

A person's word can have value and power or it can be cheap and meaningless. Persons of integrity have a reputation for keeping their word. What creates a strong reputation for integrity is behavior that is congruent, or consistent, with what we say. People listen to those who keep their word, and people organize their own behavior around promises made. For example, when Nate told me he would plaster and paint before our party, I knew I could count on him—even though the rooms had been languishing for two years, he did not know how to plaster, and we did not have matching paint. Nate is a man of his word. He has kept his promises. If Nate had not kept his word in the past, I would not have trusted that he would fix up the rooms and would not have been willing to have the party.

When spouses keep their word to each other, predictability results, which creates security and trust. They can rely on each other. In contrast, if we do not do as we say we will, our spouse eventually feels we can't be trusted and also feels resentful about being deceived. Persons who do not keep promises may feel depressed because people do not pay attention to them, and they do not understand why they feel so ineffective. If you tell your husband, "I won't use the credit cards," and then use them again and again, he won't believe you when you make this promise again. When spouses agree to save money for a long-range goal, such as a vacation, and one spouse continues to spend, the other spouse will resent it. If a spouse agrees to travel less on business but continues to spend weeks out of town, the partner begins to feel insecure about making plans for evenings together.

DISCUSSION 4. *Ask your spouse what kind of reputation you have for keeping promises in your marriage. Are you surprised?*

Categories of Promises Couples Make

There are certain areas of responsibility about which most couples make promises:

Home maintenance: putting things away, preparing meals and cleanup, cleaning clothes, cutting grass, shoveling snow, vacuuming, dusting.

Managing money: setting spending priorities, saving for long-range goals, handling the checkbook and credit cards.

Parenting: participating in various care-giving activities, setting expected behavior standards, providing rewards and consequences for those behaviors.

Parents and other family members: how much time will be spent with each spouse's parents; what extended-family activities, vacations, holidays, and celebrations the couple will participate in; how parents or other family members will be cared for during their aging.

Managing time: clarifying when partners will be together for couple and family activities and when separate; keeping time commitments.

Managing recreation: what partners will do for fun and enjoyment together and separately.

The relationship: sharing emotions and information, sexual fidelity, managing conflict, growing as a couple.

Religion: whether and in what religion to participate, in what faith to rear children.

Other promises will be unique to your relationship, such as one partner promising to support the family while the other gets an education. Add them to the list above. You will be using the list to tell each other how satisfied you are with these areas of your life.

DISCUSSION 5. *Can you think of other areas in which couples make promises?*

You will be comfortable and satisfied when you consider how you and your spouse are handling some of the categories listed above. But you may feel anxiety about or frustration with others. If you are dissatisfied, try to understand why. It could be that (1) you have not made requests or promises, (2) one of you is not keeping promises, or (3) you disagree about how that category should be handled. As you learn to communicate more clearly by making requests, declining requests that you object to, and developing more acceptable alternatives that work for both of you, you will reduce the frustration associated with each area.

You may feel anxious as you look at the categories because of areas of conflict. You may think, "I would feel like a slave if I carried out all those promises." Or, "My partner breaks promises all the time." Take heart. As you learn to make promises that are appropriate for you, you will feel more, not less, freedom. You and your partner can learn to make promises that you are willing to keep.

Conversations about requests and promises evolve over a lifetime. As you and your partner become more aware of yourselves, you will know what to request. As you age or develop emotionally, your requests will change. Also, promises that you make during one stage of your life may no longer be comfortable in another. For instance, when a mother has young children, she may promise to stay home and provide most of the meals. As her children get older or leave home, she may want to change that promise.

Some promises may be unspoken. It is better to state these agreements openly so that you have the same understanding. You do not need to use formal language, such as "I promise you that. . . . " What is important is that every time you indicate that you will do something, you intend to do it, just as you would keep a promise. Nate and I have made promises: Nate washes sheets and towels. I shop for groceries unless Nate chooses to. Nate empties the garbage into the compost pile. I maintain bank records and checkbooks. Each of us promises to care for the other's children as we would our own. Nate promised to take me out on a date once a month.

This last promise is new and I need more experience with it before I'll trust that he'll keep it. When your partner makes a promise that requires a change in behavior, it is usual not to trust it until you find out whether the partner will keep it. You need to experience the new behavior before you know you can depend on it.

✔ **EXERCISE 1.**

    1. **You will be rating, independently of each other, your level of satisfaction about making and keeping promises for each kind of promise listed on pages 151–152. In your journals, each should list the categories of promises.**

    2. **Next to the list you will record your level of satisfaction with promises in each category. The range is from 1 through 5, with 1 meaning intense dissatisfaction and 5 meaning strong trust and satisfaction with the partnership in this area. Your level of satisfaction is your subjective estimate. A number makes it easier to discuss with your spouse areas that you think need improvement. For example, if you have no plan for how to spend money, have a lot of credit card debt, and spend more money than you make each month, you are probably dissatisfied with "Managing money." However, if you manage your income so that expenses are covered, you do not accumulate debt, you have adequate money for some fun, and you have only minor disagreements about how to spend your money, you are probably satisfied.**

3. After you have both rated your lists, share them with each other. Discuss what you learned about your relationship from this exercise.

4. For each item you rated 3 or above, write one promise you or your spouse has made. Some promises may be unspoken agreements. You will discover that you are satisfied in areas of your relationship because you have kept promises in those areas, even though you may not have talked together about it. It is useful to make these agreements open and clear. Open discussion provides the groundwork for change in promises as families grow and the members have different needs. Change that meets the needs of both partners will need to be discussed openly.

5. Postpone your discussion about low-rated categories of promises. You will discuss them later, after you have learned about confronting unkept promises.

Making Good Promises

It is easiest to keep a promise if you have made a good promise in the first place. A good promise has three requirements: (1) It must be clear. (2) It must be consistent with your values. (3) You must have an adequate strategy for accomplishing it.

A Clear Promise

A clear promise states what will be done, who will do it, and by when. This may seem simple, but when most people say they will do something, they leave some parts of the agreement vague. There is a lot of room for misunderstanding about what will be done and the time frame for completion. A clear promise also sets a clear goal for the promiser to use for organizing. For example, Nate promised, "I'll work with you so that together we spend no more than $150 for food, entertainment, and household expenses a week." Now I know what Nate will do. I can organize my life around this promise. When I want to buy groceries, I get money from the $150 we set aside and we stay within the budget. However, there are times we need to renegotiate this promise, such as when we need extra money to entertain guests or we go on vacation. This promise will change as children leave home or our lifestyle changes.

✔ **EXERCISE 2.**
Return to the promise you talked about in Discussion 2. Write the promise in your journal. Identify the three parts of the promise: what was to be done, who would do it, and by when.

A Promise Consistent with Your Values

The ability to make and keep promises lies in making the *right* promises. Making the right promises means making promises consistent with your values. When you have made a good promise, the promise focuses your energy and action so that you get something done that will reward you and your spouse. You have exercised your freedom to choose. You can feel freedom and excitement in keeping such a promise. When you keep your promise to be home by six o'clock to take care of your children so that your wife can go to a meeting, you have the opportunity to be alone with your children and provide for them in your own way, while at the same time your wife feels the pleasure and satisfaction of doing something important to her.

An ineffective promise conflicts with another value—something else important to you—and you will either resent doing it or be unable to do it. For example, if you have a critical deadline at work, your promise to be at home by six o'clock may cause a conflict. In this case it is better to recognize the potential conflict and offer to find a baby-sitter rather than make a promise that you will not keep or will resent.

Some people make ineffective promises because they want to immediately please their partner. They say yes too quickly to a request because they have not really evaluated what the promise will mean to them. Then they break their promise or resent that they have to do what they said they would do. Often people who do this have a childhood history of being rejected or abused, and in the marriage feel in danger of being rejected or abused if they do not immediately conform to another's demands.

DISCUSSION 6. *Was the promise you identified in Discussion 2 one that was good for you and consistent with your values? What values did the promise represent?*

A Strategy to Fulfill the Promise

You must devise a means or strategy for keeping each promise. The concept of "strategy" is useful because if a strategy does not work, you can simply examine and change it instead of blaming yourself or your spouse. We have strategies for everything we do, but we do not think of them as strategies. An effective strategy gets the results that you intend. Such a strategy may be a simple memory jogger or a complex plan. In most families there is a strategy for getting showered and dressed without running into other family members in the bathroom, for knowing what to buy at the grocery store, for paying bills, for getting the kids to bed, even for preparing to make love. You may think, "I don't have a strategy; I never thought about it," but whatever you are currently doing is your strategy, even if you have not thought it over carefully.

DISCUSSION 7. *Everyone has a strategy for getting up in the morning. Share your strategy with your spouse.*

Strategies vary in their effectiveness—some work well and others don't accomplish what you intend. Here is one couple's strategy for a Saturday evening together, as told by the husband, George. Perhaps you recognize it. Strategies are noted in parentheses.

George [on Saturday afternoon]: Let's go to the movie tonight. (This strategy did not involve planning ahead.)

Martha: We don't have a sitter.

George [with some annoyance]: Well, call a sitter. (Strategy: Let her do the work.)

Martha [with frustration]: Why don't you call the sitter? I always call the sitter. (Strategy: resist domination.)

George: Well, forget it. (Strategy: I'd rather give up than give in.)

But Martha wants to go out, so she spends a half hour on the phone because sitters are hard to find at short notice. She finally locates a friend of a friend a few miles away who is willing to baby-sit and has to be picked up before the movie. Martha has devised an effective strategy for getting a sitter.

Martha [in a pleading voice]: Let's order pizza tonight before the movie. (Strategy: whine for someone else to provide dinner.)

George: I don't want to pay for a movie and pizza, too. We're talking

$25 already. (Why can't she just put something together? he thinks. Strategy: conserve money, which does not include a request.)

By this time the five-year-old is chanting, "Pizza! Pizza!" (The five-year-old's strategy for getting pizza.)

George: I wish I hadn't brought up the movie. It would be easier to watch a videotape at home. I'd suggest that we watch a tape instead of going out, but now you have arranged the sitter and want to go. (This is a weakly offered alternative to conserve money and effort.)

Martha opens some cans of soup and makes grilled cheese sandwiches while George bathes the baby, an effective strategy for preparing dinner and preparing the baby for bed. They are tense and have little to say to each other when they leave the house.

Although the couple got dinner and went out, their strategies produced tension and frustration and did not work to provide this couple a pleasant evening out.

DISCUSSION 8. *How would you change these strategies so that this couple could leave the house happy and relaxed? Perhaps next time the husband could invite his wife for a date earlier in the week and they could decide together who would call the sitter. There are many other possibilities for effective strategies. List some other strategies.*

DISCUSSION 9. *What is* your *strategy for weekend entertainment, for whatever you do for fun? Be specific. What is your strategy for preparing routine evening meals?*

✔ **EXERCISE 3.**
1. **Each spouse should identify a request for the following weekend. The request can be related to entertainment or any other use of time. Make the request, sharing the details of what the request means to you.**

2. **Each spouse responds to the request by listening reflectively and then making a promise. Before making the promise, you may suggest alternatives, as you learned to do in chapter 8, until you identify a promise that you are willing and able to keep. When you make the promise, confirm it by specifying (1) what you will do and (2) by when you will do it. Be sure you have a strategy for fulfilling your promise. If you do not, the first step is to develop the strategy.**

Why Do People Break Promises?

When spouses do not keep promises, their partners often handle the situation emotionally. They complain, yell, criticize, or withdraw self-righteously. This is usually ineffective. It is more constructive to examine why the promise was not kept, and reconfirm or renegotiate the promise.

Promises are broken for four basic reasons.

1. *Your partner does not know how important promises are to a satisfying life.* Some people have learned that promises are not important to keep. For example, some people grow up in a family where their best option is to promise anything in order to avoid punishment. Because they are coerced into making promises, they never learn to notice whether they actually want to do what they are promising. They fail to follow through on many promises because they resent them. This behavior, carried into marriage, leads to intense distrust from the spouse. If you or your partner do not recognize the importance of promises, review "Integrity: The Power of Keeping Your Promise" (pp. 150–154) with your partner.

Perhaps you or your spouse grew up in a family where few promises were made. This may occur, for instance, when a boy lives with his mother after his parents divorce. His mother may give him whatever he wants, in an effort to make up for his loss of a father. The child has a lot of freedom very early and nothing is asked of him in return. When he marries, he expects to be able to do as he wishes without keeping promises. His partner will want him to give as well as take. If you grew up without keeping promises, you will need to learn to do so as an adult.

2. *The promise was not clear.* A clear promise identifies who, what, and when. A spouse who does not understand the agreement will not—and cannot—keep a promise. The most frequent problem with promises is that a time for completion is not given. For example, if you thought your promise was to come home immediately after you finished work regardless of how late, but your spouse understood your promise was to be home by six o'clock, there will be a mix-up and an unkept promise. Nate recently promised to order a piece of equipment that is important to me. The next day I asked if he had ordered it. He had not, but we recognized that we had not had an agreement about when he would do it. After I asked him when he would order it and he said "this morning," our problem cleared up with no criticism or nagging.

Sometimes the details of a promise can go unsaid and leave wiggle room for someone who does not want to do the job. This can happen with spouses and often happens with children. For example, a promise to clean the kitchen may mean that only the dishes get put in the dishwasher. Dirty pots and pans are left untouched, and the floor not mopped. It is important to clarify what "clean the kitchen" means.

Sometimes the "who" part of the promise is misunderstood. For instance, if you suggest, "Let's go to the play Saturday night," and your spouse responds, "That's a great idea," you could each assume the other would reserve the tickets.

3. *The promise was in conflict with your spouse's values and priorities.* When people make promises to their family, they often do not think through the promises to determine how they will affect other commitments. They agree to something and later discover it conflicts with something else or the promise is not something they want to do. It is better to decline the promise and brainstorm options than to let your family members believe that you will do something you won't.

Celeste has a demanding job that she enjoys. She promised Alex she would limit her overtime to one evening a week but found herself working more than that because the promise conflicted with her career goals. There is a conflict between Celeste's and Alex's values. The appropriate response for Celeste would be to tell Alex that she wants to please him, but she also wants to work overtime to be in line for promotion. She would need to decline Alex's request and brainstorm other options.

4. *Your partner did not have an adequate strategy to carry out the promise.* This means the person did not think through adequately or did not know how to carry out the promise. Sometimes both partners have an ineffective strategy.

David and Mara have been married for twenty-seven years and are paying college tuition for two children. David is a lawyer and Mara a nurse. There had always been enough household money for Mara to buy what she wanted without thinking much about it. Now they are on a limited budget. Mara promised David she would not use her credit cards. Yet she charged things every month when her money budgeted for household expenses ran out. She did not know how to stay within her budget limits. David's strategy to motivate her was to scold. She became anxious about discussing the budget, and so avoided it. Mara needed to develop a strategy for living within a budget, and David needed to confront her unkept promise respectfully.

When there is no effective strategy for keeping promises, the solution is to develop one. This may require discussing the problem until one of you thinks of something more effective, or resolving to ask someone who knows a good strategy. People to talk with about developing strategies (solving problems) are friends and relatives or, in the case of a difficult problem, an expert.

Unkept Promises

When your partner makes a promise, it helps if you are optimistic and encouraging, rather than cynical, recalling all the past broken promises. However, for any of the reasons mentioned above, spouses do break promises. Nagging or badgering someone who is not keeping a promise creates resentment and frustration for both spouses. Your goal, instead, is to create partnership and work out strategies that are mutually satisfying. The resolution process, which follows, is designed to help you confront someone who is not keeping a promise in a way that does not blame and supports the relationship. David and Mara's budget disagreement is the illustration.

David confronted Mara about not keeping her promise to stay within the budget. David felt like giving up, brooding, and withdrawing. Mara felt guilty and hopeless. The resolution process took several hours and went as follows:

Step 1. Name the promise that is not being kept and express your feelings without criticizing the other person.

David began, "Mara, I am very upset about how you run up credit card bills every month. We're increasing our debt. You promised to live within your salary so we could pay tuition from mine." With some coaching, David had learned to withhold his criticisms about her and his sense of hopelessness.

Step 2. Identify why the promise is not being kept, using one of the four reasons listed above.

Mara knew how important it is to keep promises (see reason 1), and she felt very guilty about breaking hers. Her promise about how much she would spend each month was also clear (see reason 2). Mara acknowledged that she, too, wanted to live within their limits (see reason 3). As Mara talked about her spending and David listened, they discovered that Mara spent money when she felt lonely. The children were away and Mara and David frequently worked different schedules. The problem was reason number 4: Mara did not have a strategy for controlling her spending when she was lonely.

Step 3. Begin the negotiation process by affirming each person's right to have his or her own experience.

Mara and David acknowledged each other's feelings by using reflective listening. Mara could recognize David's distress about increased debt. David could understand Mara's loneliness, which resulted in spending.

Step 4. Think of options that might lead to a new promise.

Mara and David thought of many options: Mara could ask for a raise; Mara could stop using any credit cards; they could ask the children to go to state colleges that would cost less; and they could move to a less expensive house. Included in the options were ways of spending time together and ways David could communicate more respect to Mara.

Step 5. Select an option for satisfying both spouses, and make a new promise.

After much discussion, Mara and David made several new promises. They promised to spend one morning a week together. If Mara felt particularly lonely, she promised she would call David at work or call a friend instead of going shopping. David promised to speak respectfully to Mara about her spending. Mara renewed her promise not to use credit cards.

In complex situations, such as this one, spouses need to continually refine the strategy until the system works. The process of refinement will be effective if the partners continue to address the problem respectfully and do not fall into old patterns of blame and hopelessness.

Over the life of a relationship, partners use experience to predict the behavior they can expect from their spouses. David's hopelessness was, in part, a result of Mara's breaking her promise many times. When promises have been made and broken frequently, the person breaking the promise feels guilty while the spouse feels anxiety and resentment. These feelings can lead to a miserable life together or divorce. But I have seen spouses who habitually broke promises suddenly see the light and make a change so that they could learn to keep their word. In other cases, the partner had the patience to give the spouse one last chance. Sometimes, however, partners gave up because they were not willing to face another broken promise. Clearly, making and keeping promises is an important foundation to a secure marriage. With years of anticipating promises and having them fulfilled, a relationship grows secure. The couple feels like an effective team. Each feels loved. It is these daily promises we keep that fulfill our promise at our wedding to love and honor for a lifetime.

✔ **EXERCISE 4.**

Identify with your spouse an area in your relationship where a promise is not being kept. Agree which promise you will use during this exercise. Go through the steps in "Unkept Promises" with your partner.

For Practice

List the categories of promises you or your spouse rated a 1 or 2 (low satisfaction with promise keeping) in Exercise 1. Choose one of the most important categories (to either of you) and talk about the problem. Decide what needs to be done, whether one of you needs to make a request, make a promise, or keep a promise. If a promise is not being kept, go through the procedure for confronting an unkept promise. Continue through your list until you have effective promises for the entire list. Be patient. This could take weeks or months.

Chapter Ten

Feelings Communicate Meaning

Feelings direct us to what is most important in our relationship and life. Sharing feelings means saying what you feel without blaming your partner or expecting a particular response. We have feelings about events and objects that have personal meaning. Feelings can enliven a loving and creative spirit or can lead us to destroy relationships and ourselves. This chapter will help you understand emotions, which may reduce the fear and anxiety some people associate with feeling emotions, and will enhance your ability to share emotions and increase intimacy.

If you or your spouse has feelings that overwhelm you and prevent you from expressing them constructively, or if either of you is distressed by a particular feeling like anger or depression, seek psychotherapy.

Feelings Change after Marriage

Before marriage, conversation and feelings are usually about safe subjects—friends, college activities, family members, special interests, and career plans. In fact, couples often say, "We could talk very well before we got married." After marriage, the potential for negative feelings arises because partners occupy so much of each other's lives. No longer are problems external to the relationship. Rather, many problems are *about* the relationship. If we perceive our spouse as sympathetic and supportive in solving the problems, we feel much happier about the relationship. But if we perceive our spouse as an unsympathetic person who puts up barriers blocking access to things that are important to us, we can feel angry, hopeless, distant, and, eventually, unloved and unloving.

A normal source of emotions and tension in all marriages is the need for individual identity and for intimacy, or togetherness. Family therapists Michael E. Kerr and Murray Bowen suggest that these forces are biological and affect all individuals and family units.[1] When a relationship encompasses *both* individual identities and intimacy, it can be supportive, cooperative, and flexible. But if a couple cannot allow both of these needs to be met, the relationship can become out of balance and focused on negative emotions such as anger, resentment, and depression.

Feelings, in themselves, are never a problem, although most people perceive them to be. Feelings do not harm anything. Instead, it is the ineffective expression of feelings that is harmful. Couples get divorced because they do not know how to handle feelings, not because they have them. To be effective in handling feelings, partners must (1) be able to notice, or identify, what they are feeling and express the words for the feelings, and (2) not blame their spouse for their own feelings. They must understand that their feelings belong to them and are not caused by their spouse.

People rarely have one clear feeling but, instead, have a mixture of positive and negative feelings. In a close relationship, all important feelings should be shared because they identify the depth and complexity of issues and promote better problem solving and a greater degree of intimacy.

How to Express Your Feelings

Expressing feelings occurs in two steps. The first thing to do when you are coping with intense feelings is to think of words that reflect what you feel inside. This is easier for some than others. Extroverts often recognize their feelings while they talk about them. Introverts may need to remove themselves from people for a while to reflect or write about what they feel.

The second step is to share the feeling with someone you trust. Talk about the events that triggered your feeling, and your thoughts, values, and beliefs surrounding the feeling. As you learn positive communication skills, the person you share with will most often be your spouse, simply because you will be talking to each other more than ever before. As I noted, when you first met, sharing feelings as well as sharing other aspects of your lives probably felt very good. Those good feelings can return. Sharing produces growth and healing because when we share our feelings and are accepted, we do not feel isolated and alone; we feel love. Love and healing can occur whether we share positive or negative feelings. The key requirement is that the listener accepts us.

You have learned how to express positive feelings as appreciation (see chapter 7). But it is equally important to share negative feelings. It is easier, of course, to hear someone share positive feelings than negative, but it is essential to personal development as well as to your relationship that you hear and accept the negative. Trust increases when you can express negative emotions to your spouse and have those feelings understood.

Many people can listen effectively if their partner is upset about something other than them—about their job, for example, their parents, or the neighbors. But most of us have trouble listening when we are the object of the negative feelings, especially of anger. Reflective listening is the answer. In chapter 6 you learned how to use reflective listening when your partner expresses intense emotions. Even if your partner does not participate in this Recreating Marriage course, your partner can learn from your example how to express feelings and listen to you.

Avoiding Blame

The way you express feelings can make a big difference in your spouse's response. It is easier for your partner to listen if you avoid blaming him or her for your feelings. When you communicate your feelings, you should not imply that your feelings are the other person's fault. *Other people do not cause your feelings*. Rather, your feelings are a signal about your personal relationship to the event. The cause for your feelings is inside of you.

Unfortunately, most people sound as if they are blaming when they express negative feelings such as anger. It is common to express anger in personal terms. The most important mistake you can make is to call someone a name or describe character. These remarks usually begin with "You are _____." Keep in mind how important our identities are (see chapter 2), and that by name calling, couples can take a simple conflict and escalate the conversation into a war. Examples of such name-calling statements are the following: "You are irresponsible, undependable, and childish." "You are lazy and selfish." "You are stupid and insensitive." The favorites among couples in my practice are "irresponsible" and "self-centered." People often think they are sharing their feelings if they say, "*I feel* that you are irresponsible and inconsiderate," or whatever negative characteristic comes to mind, but this kind of remark is still a criticism of character even though it contains the words, "I feel. . . ." Communicating a feeling effectively requires that you focus on the behavior at hand and not attack your spouse's—or anyone else's—character.

Instead of name calling, learn and follow the simple process described in the next paragraph. It is particularly useful in expressing negative feelings without blaming or name calling, but is also helpful for sharing all feelings. Even if you are not blaming your partner, however, she or he may interpret your message as blaming, because blame is so common. It may help if you state openly that you are not blaming your partner as the conversation develops. Don't forget to use reflective listening when your partner reacts.

When you share your feelings, express them by (1) *saying what happened* and (2) *giving your response* to that event. You should say simply, "You (or he, she, they) did _____ and I feel _____. For example, "You took the checkbook from my purse and I feel angry." You can go into detail at this point about how you were inconvenienced or what you might have feared. You can ask questions about your partner's reasons or point of view. But at no time should you discredit your partner.

Remember that it is as important to express positive feelings as negative ones. In a busy life, this is easy to forget. Relationships can sustain a lot of conflict if they also contain generous amounts of positive expression.

Expressing Feelings

The two conversations that follow are models of expressing feelings and responding to one's partner. In Conversation 1, Angie and Joe, a young couple with a baby, express their feelings in a way that leads to no resolution and leaves wounds. In this situation, Angie is angry with Joe when he leaves her with their young baby so he can go out with his friends. In the exercise that follows, you will identify why Joe and Angie feel the way they do, and you will also examine some reasons for your own feelings. This should give you more precision in naming your feelings and ways to care for your feelings. You are each responsible for taking care of your own feelings.

Begin by reading the conversation silently.

Conversation 1.

Joe left a message for Angie at four o'clock that he planned to go out with his volleyball friends after work. Joe had been working a lot of overtime and felt he needed a break. Angie worked part-time while Joe's mother cared for their daughter, Jill. Angie felt overburdened caring for a young child. She rarely went out except to buy groceries and supplies. Her only time away from her daughter was at work. When she learned that Joe was going out with friends, she felt very angry. Her anger built during the evening as she ate dinner alone and waited for Joe to return. He came in at about eight thirty. As Joe took off his coat, Angie's smoldering anger burst out.

Angie: Joe, you went out with your friends instead of coming home. You know I need to see you in the evenings. I think it's irresponsible of you not to come home! You're working a lot now and you aren't around! I think you like to escape into your work. You didn't even find out if I needed you! You just left the message on the tape! You're inconsiderate!

Joe *hates* it when his wife is angry or disappointed in him. He does not know what to say, but his anger brews. He turned the T.V. on to quiet down a little, hoping she would stop yelling. Instead, Angie was incensed by his further avoidance.

Angie: Now you're going to watch T.V. instead of talking to me. You never talk to me. You never go out with me. You go out with your friends. You play volleyball! You're very selfish!

Joe [unable to hold his anger in any longer]: You harp on me all the time. I work hard all day and come home to your complaints!

Angie: Well, you didn't work hard all day today!

Eventually Angie went to bed. Joe watched television until he was sure she was asleep before he went to bed.

✔ **EXERCISE 1.**

   1. **After silently reading Conversation 1, read it aloud with each other, the wife reading for Angie and the husband for Joe.**

   2. **Discuss how this conversation could have been improved.**

   3. **Now read aloud Conversation 2, below, with each partner reading one of the roles. Conversation 2 is a replay of the same circumstances and feelings, but this time the couple express themselves effectively.**

   4. **After reading, identify the communication steps that moved the couple from anger to a hug. Discuss this before reading further.**

Conversation 2.

When Joe came home late after an evening with friends, Angie shared her feelings, yelling at Joe.

Angie: Joe, you went out with your friends after work and I feel very angry. I worked all day and looked forward to spending time with you and Jill. I felt so disappointed you didn't come home after work. In fact, you've been working so much recently that I feel lonely a lot.

Although Joe *hates* it when Angie is angry or disappointed with him, he has learned to use reflective listening effectively, because he knows it produces better results than if he yells at Angie.

Joe: You're really mad at me for going out tonight.

Angie: Yeah, I *am* feeling exhausted taking care of Jill and working. I'm feeling that you're too busy for us. We don't have fun any more.

Angie appreciated that he heard her. She recognized that she was complaining and turned her complaint into a request.

Angie: I request that we go out together Friday night. I'd like to make it a long evening like we used to have. Dinner and a play. How does that sound to you?

Joe agreed in principle, but came he back with a more acceptable alternative.

Joe: I'm so beat when Friday comes, I'd like to stay home and crash in front of a video. But Saturday would be a great time to go out, if you think you can wait that long.

Now Angie had something to look forward to and she was relieved. Her anger melted.

Angie: I'll call for tickets. Can you ask your mom to baby-sit? (They had never left their baby in the evening. Joe agreed to ask his mom.)

Angie [confiding other feelings]: I'm so lonely sometimes, just being with our baby long hours. I think I need to have some activities of my own, or take Jill out to do something. There's a reading group for mothers with babies at the library I'd like to find out about. Also, Marie's been asking me out for lunch. I'd like to see her some time.

Joe [recognizing Angie was over her anger and deciding to share his own feelings]: You know, Angie, when I came home and you were mad at me, I felt really misunderstood. I felt like you didn't appreciate how hard I work and how much stress I feel.

Angie [realizing it was now her turn to use reflective listening]: You felt upset that I didn't appreciate how hard you work. You think you deserve a break.

Joe: That's it. And I hate it when you're angry with me. (He was feeling encouraged by her response and could express a bit more.)

Angie: When I'm mad at you, you just can't stand it.

Joe: Yes. I think I'm doing the best that I can and then I come home and I get pounded. At least, now I know how to listen and you calm down. Not like my parents who argued all the time.

Angie [reflecting]: My anger reminds you of your parents' fighting. But you're relieved we don't get into blowups all the time.

Joe: Yes! I'm glad you understand. (He hugged her.)

Moving from the kind of interaction illustrated by Conversation 1 to the kind illustrated by Conversation 2 takes practice. There were three important differences in the first and the second conversation. First, in the second conversation, but not the first, Angie and Joe believed that they could be effective with each other. We know that because they started off with less anger and they had more purpose in their behavior. When people have confidence that they can be effective, they are less angry. Second, they blamed each other in the first conversation; they accepted responsibility for themselves in the second. They looked for solutions in the second conversation instead of attempting to identify the culprit. And third, they used reflective listening in the second conversation but not the first. At this point in your Recreating Marriage course, embrace the belief that you, too, can be effective in communicating with your partner.

✔ **EXERCISE 2.**
1. **Review tables 7–2 and 8–1 (pp. 114 and 140) and use them to identify your own feelings.**

2. **Take turns expressing to each other a negative feeling that one of you has had about the other, using the pattern, "You did _____, and I felt _____."**

3. **Listen reflectively to your partner's feelings.**

4. **Take turns expressing to each other a positive feeling one of you has had about the other, using the pattern, "You did _____, and I felt _____."**

5. **Listen reflectively to your partner's feelings.**

Why Do We Have Feelings?

Feelings are a natural part of being human. Emotions such as sexual attraction, the attachment between a mother and infant, empathy with members of one's group, competition for territory and resources, and probably the emotions that grow out of the need for intimacy and for a separate identity have helped human beings survive on earth. God gave us these emotions through our nervous and hormonal systems. Emotions are caused by chemical reactions in our brain and nervous system that send messages through nerves and hormones to communicate with all the cells of the body. When we are aware of our emotional experience, we refer to it as a feeling. How we act on our emotions depends on what we have learned from our cultural and personal history.

But beyond these human and cultural reasons, we have personal feelings for specific reasons. Feelings benefit us in many ways. We can enrich our lives if we notice, savor, and communicate pleasure. When we are in pain, it helps to know why we are hurting. When you notice a strong feeling, look for the message of your feeling. What is the purpose of that feeling? Remember: Solve the problem; don't blame the person.

Feelings play six roles in people's lives:

1. *Feelings identify what is important to us—our values and beliefs.*

We have feelings about anything that has personal meaning—those events and objects that represent our identity, values, and beliefs. People cannot possibly pay attention to everything, and feelings are a way of sorting out what to pay attention to. Spouses function effectively when they acknowledge that their feelings, opinions, values, beliefs, and ways of doing things are separate from the partner's, and recognize that the differences have to be explored and negotiated through communication.

Remember the idea of alignment, discussed in chapter 2? Our feelings can signal when we are living in alignment with our identity, values, and beliefs. We feel happy and have a sense of well-being when we are true to ourselves. Some people experience this as a feeling of "doing God's will." Others may call it peace of mind or serenity. Spending an evening helping your children with homework can feel satisfying because you are participating in relationships and activities that you value. Similarly, finishing a project at work, making a meal, or watching a sports event with your spouse will feel satisfying if those actions are consistent with your values.

If your important values are not being fulfilled, you will be distracted, and you would not enjoy time spent in doing homework with your children, making that meal, or watching the sports event. When an experience is in conflict with your identity, values, or beliefs, you feel negative emotions. You feel as if something of significant value, such as a job or a relationship, is in danger or lost. You may notice unpleasant feelings such as anxiety, resentment, anger, or sadness. You can use negative emotions like these to alert you to take action, to resolve issues and solve problems, and thus return to internal harmony.

You can better communicate when you understand what your feelings mean. When you can identify the value or belief that is in conflict with your experience or being neglected, you can speak about your own experience rather than blaming your partner. Other people can then understand you and are less likely to feel blamed for your discomfort. If you communicate the issues clearly, you can seek appropriate solutions to problems.

In the course of our marriage, Nate and I experience many feelings. I list a few below and explain their importance to us. Use this list to identify more completely your own feelings.

1. I feel happy when my children are successful because successful children support my identity of "good mother."

2. I feel angry when someone makes a put-down remark about women because put downs about women reflect negatively on my identity as a woman.

3. I feel upset when the house is disorganized and dirty because a disorganized and dirty house violates my value of beauty.

4. Nate feels irritated when we do not shovel ice off the steps because he holds a belief that icy steps are dangerous to our family.

When we value something, we are pleased and happy when that value is fulfilled and we are upset and frustrated when the value is denied.

Mark is unhappy with his job because his boss's behavior clashes with Mark's values of cooperation and support on a team. Mark likes to help people solve their problems. He feels great satisfaction both in working with his church youth group and in solving employee problems at work. Mark works as a personnel manager for a man who dominates, criticizes, and demeans his employees. Mark is strong enough to stand up to the man, and also tries to support his colleagues and to help them negotiate with their boss. When he is unsuccessful in helping them to resolve their conflicts with their boss, he feels so angry and resentful toward his boss that he considers leaving his job. His values about human relationships at work are being denied.

It is natural to have mixed emotions when more than one value affects a particular situation. All your feelings can be expressed; they do not need to be consistent. You do not need to express yourself logically or rationally. Your mind knows what needs to be said, and you can trust it. You can sort out mixed emotions by talking with and listening reflectively to each other. As demonstrated in chapter 2, people can be torn or undecided about how to play their various roles. For example, you may feel joy over the birth of a child and at the same time feel the loss of freedom and have anxiety about being a new parent. Or an event as sad as the death of a parent can be mixed with relief that the parent is no longer suffering.

Feelings can also identify that a belief is being challenged. We are comfortable when people around us support our beliefs, but when our beliefs are not upheld, we can feel angry, depressed, or anxious. I believe Nate and I need a budget to manage our money. I feel secure when we spend within our budget. When we ignore the budget and spend too much money from time to time, I feel anxious. My anxiety tells me something important—that I should get back on the budget.

Important decisions should incorporate the values and beliefs of both spouses. This means that couples should express feelings about everything about which they make decisions and promises, such as what to spend money on, where to live, how to use their time, and how to raise children (see chapter 9, "Categories of Promises Couples Make"). When partners express their values and negotiate their differences, they maintain a balance between safeguarding their individual identities and nurturing intimacy, both of which are critical ingredients of a happy marriage.

DISCUSSION 1. *Review the two conversations between Angie and Joe, and identify some of their values.*

✔ **EXERCISE 3.**
  List three of your important values in your journal. Describe your feelings about each value, using tables 7–2 and 8–1 on pages 114 and 140.

DISCUSSION 2. *Think about a time when you felt a positive emotion— pleasure, joy, happiness, pride, for example. Think a moment about the value or belief that underlay the experience you enjoyed. Tell your spouse about the moment of pleasure and the value.*

DISCUSSION 3. *Think about a time when you felt negative emotions such as anger, disappointment, frustration, or hurt. What belief or value felt threatened or violated? Tell your spouse about that incident and the value.*

DISCUSSION 4. *Tell your spouse about an incident in which you had a strong, pleasant feeling about him or her. See if you can identify the value or belief that your spouse was supporting at the time you felt so good.*

DISCUSSION 5. *Identify an incident in which you felt a strong negative feeling toward your spouse. Identify the value or belief with which your spouse's behavior was in conflict. Tell your spouse about this.*

2. Sharing feelings is the basis of intimacy.
Many partners think their spouse just *knows* what they feel. This is a mistake. Clients tell me exasperating stories about such misunderstandings, and I ask them, "Did you tell your wife (or husband) what you were feeling?" Frequently the person tells me, "My wife knows how I feel."

You may have told your partner on other occasions what you were feeling, but your partner does not know what you are feeling *now* unless you have communicated that. Do not assume that your spouse knows how you feel about something. You have a unique blend of personal history, values, and beliefs. What you are feeling at any particular time cannot be predicted so easily. You must express yourself to be fully understood.

Because feelings tell us how a thing or event affects our identity, sharing feelings is the basis of intimacy. Telling a spouse about the feelings that are most important communicates trust and vulnerability and honors the partner. And because emotions signify what is important, spouses want to know how their partners feel. Feelings show us that our partner is connected to us. An invisible bond links us, even in the midst of hurt and pain. In fact, it is because of the bond that we feel the pain. If there were no connection, our partner could do anything and we would have no feelings about it. Some people think they do not love the spouse because they are angry at the spouse all the time. They are angry precisely because they do feel deeply connected and, therefore, deeply hurt.

Telling your spouse how you feel will make your partner feel like a special person, deeply connected to you. It is important to express feelings about everything you care about. This does not mean you can behave in an intimidating or frightening way. You must communicate your feelings effectively, in a way that does not blame and seeks to solve problems. As you become accustomed to talking about ordinary feelings, you will feel closer to each other. And if talking about feelings becomes a habit, an intense emotional experience will not disrupt your connection.

Maintaining the balance between individual identity and intimacy can be affected by one additional issue. Sometimes love is mistaken for agreement. Love and agreement are not the same thing. When partners are not able to express and negotiate their differences, it may indicate that one person wants much more individuality or intimacy than the other. Joe, in our example, may think that Angie wants too much of his time and so he is beginning to draw away from her. Angie is already feeling abandoned. Over the years, if one person draws away and the other feels abandoned, the feeling of love will diminish, and resentment, anger, and depression will increase until feelings toward a spouse die. You can see that if Angie and Joe are unable to talk about what is important to them, their relationship will feel unsatisfying and the negative feelings will prevent them from experiencing love.

Some people have trouble expressing feelings. Often one of two reasons is the cause, and both reasons are related to our experiences as children. In the first case, a person may have grown up in a family that was not fluent in the language of emotions, so no one talked about feelings. In the second, a person may have grown up in a family in which sharing feelings was frightening or dangerous and made the person vulnerable. Some people grew up with parents who criticized, attacked, or punished their children for openly saying what they felt. Often people who grew up with an alcoholic parent are afraid to say what they feel because the parent easily lost emotional control. The person wants to avoid vulnerability, the very thing that creates intimacy. People can overcome fear of vulnerability if their spouse will listen reflectively whenever the hesitant partner speaks about anything. A spouse who listens reflectively sends the message, "It is safe to tell me your feelings."

Although learning to express emotions may not be difficult once you have learned the language to name different feelings, learning the language is all important—and even intelligent people can be emotionally illiterate.

Jacob is an astrophysicist, married to Carol, a psychologist. Carol urged him to go to therapy in order to learn to express his feelings, and he wanted to do this to please his wife. It is not unusual for a man to come to therapy as a result of a wife's complaint that he does not express feelings. Jacob did not seem to have any particular reason to fear his feelings. He had no emotional traumas lurking in his memory, and he seemed to have a pleasant and affectionate relationship with his wife.

I asked him to describe some of his feelings—about anything—but he could not think of any. I suggested that we make a list of feelings, just to find out if he knew what feelings were. We did that, both contributing to the list. I asked him if he could recall having any of these feelings, and he could easily provide examples of experiencing some of the feelings on our list. He just had not been identifying his feelings most of the time. He took the list home and wrote the feelings on a note card that he could carry with him to help identify what he was feeling. During the next week he told Carol when he was having particular feelings. Recognizing his feelings and telling her about them seemed miraculous to them. At his next session, Jacob reported that Carol was happy with what he had learned, and as a result, she felt closer to him. Motivation and education worked very well in this case.

DISCUSSION 6. *Identify the feelings that Angie and Joe express in Conversations 1 and 2 on pages 166–167 and 167–168. How does expressing feelings contribute to the emotional distance and closeness between them, as it is portrayed in their two conversations? How do you know when they are distant or close?*

DISCUSSION 7. *Identify a time in your marriage when you felt very close to your partner. What was happening? What were your feelings? Use tables 7–2 and 8–1 on pages 114 and 140 to help you identify feelings. Tell your spouse about it.*

DISCUSSION 8. *Identify a time when you wanted to feel closer to your spouse. What was happening? What were your feelings? Use tables 7–2 and 8–1 to help you identify feelings. Tell your spouse about it.*

3. Feelings motivate us.

Feelings can encourage us to take action, to accomplish what we value, to act in our best interest. Positive feelings such as desire, confidence, courage, and determination strengthen our resolve to conquer obstacles and keep going. They signal that we are going in the right direction.

Feelings are not always positive, however, and negative feelings can subdue motivation and discourage a person from taking action. The absence of motivation says, "This event or object is not an important part of my identity," which means that it is in conflict with a belief or value. If you notice that you have no motivation to engage in a particular activity, ask yourself, "Which of my values is in conflict with this activity?" If you are forcing yourself to do something that conflicts with an important value, you will be much happier and more motivated if you change your activities so that your important values are reflected in them.

Liz, a mother of three boys, longed to paint. She loved her children and cared for them well, but she felt severely depressed because she was not using her mind creatively. Part of her identity was being an artist, yet she was not being one. Whenever she found a moment to herself and tried to paint, she was soon interrupted by a child's need, quarrels among children, or the need to make a meal.

She talked with her husband about how demoralized she felt doing nothing but taking care of the house and children. He supported her desire to set aside several hours each day to paint. This required making arrangements for someone to take care of the children on a regular basis. Her husband had to prepare some meals and help with housework. At first, Liz felt guilty. Paying for child care stressed their limited budget and her work produced no income. She wondered if honoring her values was worth disrupting the family.

Although she stuck with her painting, she experienced conflict over her decision. It was two years before she let herself take her painting seriously and felt comfortable releasing her family responsibilities to other people. She applied to and was accepted by a prestigious art school. When she became more active in her creative work, she was happy to juggle time with her children, prepare meals, and manage some household duties.

Sometimes we convince ourselves that obstacles are impossible to overcome. This kind of ineffective belief can discourage motivation and action and can lie behind depression, frustration, and demoralization. One of the most demoralizing beliefs is a variation of "I am inadequate" or "I am not attractive enough, don't make enough money, or am not intelligent enough, talented enough, tall enough, thin enough, or strong enough . . . to accomplish my goals (which grow out of values)." The solution to this ineffective belief is to change it. It takes time and persistence, but it can be done. To change an ineffective belief, do three things:

1. Tell your spouse about your intention to change it.

2. Identify in your journal a value you want to honor and how to accomplish that goal, and write the affirmative prayer, "With God's help, I can. . . ." Say this prayer daily and ask your spouse to affirm you daily.

3. Cultivate friends with whom you have an affirmative relationship.

In chapter 7 you learned how to motivate people positively, using appreciation and praise. When you motivate positively, you add to the pleasure and effectiveness of your partnership because your partner retains his or her individuality while pleasing you. The opposite kind of motivation is use of complaints, nonverbal communication of disapproval, and unpleasant emotions such as your anger or misery to convince your partner to do what you want. You can even intimidate your partner with threats to leave or do harm. This kind of behavior may get what you want temporarily, but it destroys trust and goodwill and eventually will destroy your relationship. If either partner uses intimidation to motivate the other, seek counseling.

DISCUSSION 9. *In Conversations 1 and 2, what feelings seem to be motivating Angie and Joe (see pp. 166–167 and 167–168)? What does each of them believe? Are their beliefs effective in getting what they want?*

✔ **EXERCISE 4.**
Write in your journal about a time when you felt strongly motivated. What were your feelings? What were your values? What were your beliefs? Share these feelings with your spouse.

4. Emotions make us feel alive.

Feeling alive means responding to the world. The ever-flowing change in emotions is invigorating. But in order to feel invigorated by feelings rather than frightened by them, you need two skills. First, you need to recognize that feelings change when they are expressed to a receptive listener. Acknowledging and expressing feelings allows them to change as your awareness of events in your life changes. People will empathize with you and share their knowledge and wisdom with you in return. Second, you need to know how to express feelings constructively. You may express your feelings verbally, physically, or through artistic expression, but for our purposes here, verbal expression of feelings between spouses is the crucial means of communication.

It is empowering to believe that we *have* our emotions, rather than that we *are* our emotions. Emotions change; they are not part of your identity. How often have you characterized yourself by your emotions thinking, "I am an anxious (courageous, happy, depressed, or whatever) person." This may make you feel stuck with emotions that you do not want. When you characterize yourself as an emotion—"I am an anxious person," for instance—you intensify your awareness of that emotion. You notice your anxiety, primarily, and do not notice the other emotions you feel. Notice, instead, under which circumstances you *have* particular feelings. You can cope better with unpleasant feelings if you know that they change. You may have noticed that when you told someone you were angry or afraid, the feeling passed. If a wound is deep and painful, however, you may need to express the feelings to a receptive listener many times before healing occurs.

Some people always seem to express a narrow range of feelings or a single emotion, often depression or anger. People who are stuck with one emotion often have difficulty fully expressing that feeling to a receptive listener. Whenever they try to express the feeling, such as anger, well-meaning friends and relatives try to talk them out of it or they avoid the person altogether, thereby denying him or her the opportunity to talk. Anyone who has intense and unchanging feelings should seek a counselor to help solve the complex problems that are causing the discomfort.

It is normal for emotions to change during the course of a day—in fact, during the course of several minutes! Notice in the example below how many times my experiences and feelings changed during one morning—by only 8:30 A.M.

I woke up barely remembering Nate coming to bed after he returned from California. I felt happy to snuggle with him. Then I remembered I had missed him a lot this week and felt sad about his absence. I realized he was spending as much time in California as at home. I considered that he could even have another family in California. I told him about my thoughts and my sadness. He laughed and said he worked such long hours in California that he did not have time for another family. He was warm and obviously happy to be with me. I felt comforted.

As we were getting dressed, Nate complained that the kids and I had not shoveled the snow from the steps and walk. He seemed quite irritated, and described graphically how my life would be affected if I broke my hip or wrist slipping on the steps. I said that I had brushed the snow off with a broom. He said it was not done adequately and the steps were quite icy—it would only take thirty seconds to clean them properly. I told him it took me five minutes, and that I do not feel a commitment to do a better job on the steps. I felt irritated and distant from him. I went downstairs to eat breakfast and comfort myself.

After breakfast, Nate drove me to an early morning meeting at church. We teased each other about shoveling sidewalks and I felt playful. I looked forward to seeing friends, sharing our spiritual journeys, and praying. On a whim, a group member, Ruth, had brought two books to recommend to us. One was *A Year in Provence*, by Peter Mayle, a description of a couple living in that region of France. As it happens, Nate and I were to be vacationing there the next week, and I was looking for a book to whet my appetite for the trip. The second book was *Neversink*, by Leonard M. Wright Jr., stories of Wright's catching and losing fish, his efforts to improve the fabled Neversink stream in the Catskills, and his experiments with raising hybrid strains of trout. It would be a perfect present for Jonathan, my stepson, the passionate fisherman in the family who was having a birthday in two weeks. I marveled at finding these special treasures at just the moment I needed them. Then I told the group about one of my clients, a mother whose child was schizophrenic. The mother was blaming and punishing herself. We discussed how we might bring God's forgiveness to those who do not believe in it. I felt enriched and supported by my friends. From there I went to my office.

Not all of my feelings that morning were "happy," but each was a step in my day and a response to my life. As you recognize and share your feelings, your life and your relationship with your spouse will feel richer. You will gain confidence in your feelings instead of trying to avoid them and you will expand your vocabulary in describing the nuances of feelings.

DISCUSSION 10. *Describe how Angie's and Joe's feelings changed from the beginning to the end of each conversation (see pp. 166–167 and 167–168). Why do you think their feelings changed as they did during these conversations?*

✔ **EXERCISE 5.**

List in your journal some things you did today. Name the feeling you had with each experience. If you do not remember what you felt, visualize yourself in the experience and notice what you feel right now as you think about it. Consult tables 7–2 and 8–1 on pages 114 and 140 to remind you of some choices.

Tell your spouse about an event in your day and your feelings about the event.

5. Emotions create continuity with the past.

Events that trigger emotions are important even though they may seem ordinary. Everyday life events or special occasions can evoke powerful emotions. Family events may invite feelings associated with happy memories. Going to a familiar beach may be comforting and pleasant. The smell of saltwater, the sounds of seabirds, sun on your face, and sand in your toes may evoke a rush of good memories.

Often an event will trigger a memory of an earlier, similar experience about which we had a strong feeling. In such cases, not only do we feel the present event, but the feelings associated with the previous event flood back. The earlier event often occurred in childhood, and the associated feelings can be positive or negative. I often cry in church singing certain hymns. I spent many hours in church sitting beside my parents. It was some of the most intimate time we shared as a family. The old hymns put me right back beside them in Petal Methodist Church, and I weep for the miles and time between us now.

Not all memories, however, are positive. Take mealtimes, for instance. How your original family participated in family meals can affect your feelings about eating with your spouse and children. Some families quarrel and dig at each other at the table. For others, Mom's dinners were the high point of the day. You can feel pleasant anticipation at the idea of sitting down together or a knot of fear in the pit of your stomach, depending on your early experience. If your present family meals and those of your original family are unpleasant, tell your spouse about your memories. Then you and your spouse can plan a way to have meals that does not repeat your unpleasant memories.

When couples share memories and feelings, their relationship grows closer. Sharing fond memories includes your spouse in your past life. Talking about past hurtful events and the feelings produced by them can help you release the discomfort so that the negative feeling does not keep repeating itself. In time, most uncomfortable feelings about memories will clear up from talking about them. Nate used to speak often about his "troubled childhood." Recently, he mentioned that he remembers his childhood fondly, and that his parents gave him a strong foundation. I asked, "Then your troubled childhood was a myth?" He responded with comments about how much he appreciated his childhood in rural Iowa. Nate was being genuine in both accounts of his childhood. His feelings about his memories actually changed as a result of talking about them.

In some instances problems with negative memories are not as easy to resolve. Severe childhood emotional threats can interfere with a marriage. If a child experienced an event as severely threatening, he or she can develop a rigid pattern. Traumatic events that occur once or repeatedly can affect a child. For instance, a child may perceive a threat when her parents have loud, angry arguments. She may grow up feeling uncomfortable with conflict and determined to avoid arguments. As an adult, she may feel overwhelmed during arguments and withdraw as she did during childhood, so that she avoids disagreements with her husband. Or a young boy mistreated by his father may learn that men cannot be trusted. Anything that reminds him of the behavior pattern of his father re-creates his mistrust. He may have difficulty making friends with other men, and avoid loud and strong men. Or he may incorporate the identity of his father and become like him, severely limiting his relationship with his wife and children. In each of these cases, identity is rigidly held because it was learned when the child's survival seemed threatened. If an emotion such as anger or depression persistently distresses you or your spouse, seek professional help. You will need to talk with someone who understands and is not afraid of your emotions.

DISCUSSION 11. *What events in Angie or Joe's past might be contributing to their conversations (see pp. 166–167 and 167–168)?*

DISCUSSION 12. *Share a pleasant experience from your childhood that you like to relive.*

DISCUSSION 13. *Identify a situation that usually upsets you. Try to recall incidents in your early life about which the unpleasant situation may be reminding you. Tell your spouse about the event in your past.*

6. Feelings alert us to the condition of our body.
People need to be aware of the physical condition of their body and take care of its needs. If they do that, the body can have a positive influ-

ence on their emotions. It is important to be aware of normal physiological changes, such as hunger, tiredness, or the hormonal changes of a menstrual cycle, which can affect feelings. When people are tired, for example, they often display more negative feelings. A mother who comes home after a stressful day at work and encounters her teenagers quarreling may become angry or frustrated. If the same event had occurred early on a weekend day she might have ignored it or inquired about the problem and helped them settle it. Hunger is another physical need that is closely related to emotions. We often feel hungry at times when we do not actually need food but feel sadness, anxiety, or anger. Menstrual cycle changes can magnify a woman's negative feelings or add to her sense of well-being, depending on the phase of the cycle.

More seriously, some emotional disorders, such as attention deficit disorder and some forms of depression and schizophrenia, seem to be strongly influenced by physiology. These conditions can be treated with medication and psychotherapy. If you or a member of your family has emotions that interfere with your relationships and daily life, seek professional help to diagnose the problem and determine the appropriate treatment.

You can do many things to support your body and thereby develop emotional resilience. Create a stress-management program that keeps your emotions at the level of flexible self-expression rather than in a wide range that runs from too cold to too hot. If you practice the principles of good stress management, you will feel more in control when a conflict pushes your emotional hot button.

Incorporating some or all of the following practices into your own daily stress-management program will help you lower stress and cope with difficult issues.

Physical Exercise. Your mood and your thoughts will be more positive when you exercise regularly. Exercise that increases your breathing and heart rate, and thereby the oxygen in your bloodstream, also increases the brain's natural stress-reducing chemicals. Experiment with activities that you enjoy and that fit your body type. If you are unaccustomed to physical activity, you will need a medical checkup. Work into exercise gradually. You may need to reorganize your time and other activities to fit exercise in. Although almost any physical activity can reduce stress, highly competitive persons should avoid competitive sports for the purpose of stress management. Competition actually increases the stress in these persons. Stress-reducing activities need not be limited to what you might consider athletic activities—

running and weight lifting, for instance—but can include walking through neighborhoods or hiking woodland paths, bicycling, gardening, jazzercize, swimming, or water aerobics. Some people find it motivating to belong to a health club, where a variety of exercise opportunities are provided. And if you can participate in an activity as a couple, you get the added benefit of time together.

Calming Activities. Special interests that nurture your soul also can help you reduce stress. These include meditating, reading, playing or listening to music, playing with children, sailing, camping, fishing, reading or writing poetry, writing, painting, sculpturing, playing sports, dancing, and engaging in other art forms or working on some home decorating projects. Creative activities that are not goal-related are relaxing because you will be less likely to judge your success. The activity should be enjoyed for its own sake. As you express yourself through creative activities, you will become more spontaneous and energetic. If you and your spouse can find some activities from which you both derive pleasure, the relationship as well as your own emotional health will be benefited.

Healthy Diet. People who are not adequately nourished have more emotional distress. Become informed about good nutrition. Decide for yourself what eating plan is beneficial, and follow it with flexibility so you can enjoy your favorite foods. I think of some foods as "fun foods," and I know that they do not benefit me nutritionally. I enjoy them on special occasions, but not daily.

Some people eat unhealthy food instead of expressing themselves. When they feel anxious, depressed, or angry, they comfort or distract themselves by eating, usually something high in calories. Learning skills to communicate and solve problems effectively can give alternatives to eating. You cannot address your life and relationship issues if you distract yourself by eating.

A Spiritual Practice. Developing a relationship with God can give you confidence and give your life meaning, no matter what your circumstances. People relate to God by many names and in many ways, and couples need to choose how to nurture themselves and their families spiritually. Developing your relationship with God and a religious community is a process for each person and couple to consider as a way of drawing spiritual strength and having a community to celebrate life's triumphs and grieve life's inevitable losses. Spiritual nurture takes a variety of forms: reading and meditating on what has been written by inspired persons; communication with God through prayer and listening; gathering with a community for worship; periods of abstinence (such as fasting) to get perspective on what is important; self-examination and confession; and conversations with a spiritual director, mentor, or friend. Each of these requires practice—and often training. A particularly helpful resource for the development of individual spirituality is *Soul Feast*, by Marjorie Thompson.[2]

Minimizing Alcohol Consumption and Avoiding Other Recreational Drugs. Some people can use alcohol without detrimental effects, but for others, alcohol use over time can be harmful and even devastating. It may be difficult to sort out which type you are; and many persons whose relationships suffer from the abuse of alcohol do not recognize it. Let the deciding factor here be your spouse and children, the people who live closest to you. If they say that your use of alcohol is interfering with their relationship with you, stop using it. If you cannot give up drinking in order to benefit your relationship, perhaps you do have a drinking problem. Alcoholics Anonymous groups are available in every community, and there is no longer a stigma in attending. Persons from all social groups participate. If you think your spouse has a drinking or drug problem, tell her or him your opinion, and then attend Alanon, which is for families of alcoholics. You will benefit greatly from learning how to handle your own feelings and behavior.

Alcohol and recreational drugs alter your feelings. If you use either because you are feeling intense emotional pain, go to a psychiatrist who can prescribe appropriate medication to reduce the intensity of your emotions. Many kinds of medication that will not have the detrimental effects of drugs and alcohol can enhance one's ability to cope with feelings. Your family will be very grateful.

DISCUSSION 14. *What might be happening physically to Angie and Joe that could contribute to each conversation (see pp. 166–167 and 167–168)?*

DISCUSSION 15. *Tell your spouse about a time when your emotions were affected by your physical condition.*

DISCUSSION 16. *If you think your spouse has a drinking or drug problem, find a time when you can spend a few minutes together undisturbed. Then tell your spouse. Answer any questions that your spouse asks, such as, "What makes you think that? Can you give me some examples?" Do not discuss any other issues unless your spouse indicates a willingness to do so. Handling conflicts about drinking or drug use may require many conversations and it may be necessary to seek professional help.*

Accepting Unacceptable Feelings

During our lives we learn that certain emotions are acceptable and others are not. It is a rare family that can accept all emotions and react to them effectively. We learn as children in one of two ways that certain feelings are not acceptable. In the first case, parents teach that feelings are unacceptable by directly telling their children or by avoiding the feelings themselves. For example, in some families it is unacceptable for boys to be afraid. Boys may be encouraged to face new situations with bravado and ridiculed if they show weakness. In other families it is unacceptable for a child to be angry with a parent. A child's anger may be seen as disrespect for the parent's authority. Some families value humility so much that to show pride in oneself is improper. Certainly, in many families, acknowledging sexual feelings is unacceptable. Clearly, there is no unanimous agreement among families about what emotions are acceptable. The feelings that were not permitted in your family will create discomfort for you when you experience them as an adult or your spouse expresses them.

In the second case, a feeling may have so dominated or controlled your family as you were growing up that you became determined to avoid that feeling in your adult life. For instance, if you had a parent who was always depressed, you may have said to yourself, "I never want to be sad like that." You could, as a result, develop an unwavering optimistic attitude and reject all sadness, even when feelings of sadness are warranted. Or you might have learned to fear and avoid anger if your parents had loud or physical arguments that frightened you. Nate is reluctant to acknowledge that he needs me. In fact, he has often said with pride, "I don't need anyone." He grew up in a tough farm community where real men don't need tender care (sex, of course, was a different matter). He also learned from early experience with women that he dated that he could not count on them.

It is useful, as adults, to put these childhood experiences into perspective, recognizing that it is not the feeling itself that is the problem, but the way it was handled. Nate needed encouragement to express needing or wanting me. He has come to believe gradually that he could depend on me. As you learn constructive ways to express all your feelings, you will gain confidence in your ability to share your feelings. It helps to know that, ultimately, sharing *any feeling* will create intimacy, if it is done without blaming another person. The intimacy will build over time, depending on your partner's ability to receive your emotions. Having a lively, loving relationship depends on both partners being willing and able to share themselves.

✔ **EXERCISE 6.**
Review tables 7–2 and 8–1 on pages 114 and 140. Using the tables, write two lists of feelings in your journal: (1) those feelings you are uncomfortable expressing to your spouse, but are still able to express, and (2) those feelings you are very uncomfortable expressing to your spouse, and therefore withhold.

Share your lists with your spouse. Spouses should listen reflectively, without judgment.

DISCUSSION 17. *Select one feeling that you are very uncomfortable sharing with your spouse. Discuss how that feeling became unacceptable to you. Reevaluate that feeling, and decide for yourself whether it is acceptable.*

Feelings and Personality Types

Remember the Myers-Briggs personality types? (See chapter 3.) Feelings affect people differently depending on their personality type. It is not always women who complain that their spouse is not expressive, but it seems that more women are able to reveal their feelings than men, probably because more women than men have the Feeling preference in the Myers-Briggs types. And people who have a Feeling preference, including men, are more likely to share their emotional life than are those with a Thinking preference. Men have a reputation—perhaps undeserved—for not being expressive; it may be that only those men with the Thinking preference deserve that reputation.

Couples should use behavior from both Feeling and Thinking preferences when sharing their experiences and deciding to take action. Both Thinking and Feeling types will naturally give their own preference more weight. Persons with a Thinking preference make decisions on a rational basis. They think through decisions, using primarily their beliefs and rational thought. They tend to be deliberate, analytical, and emotionally reserved. This does not mean that they have fewer emotions. They can be sensitive and emotionally reactive. However, they are less likely to know the words for their feelings, and they are reluctant to make decisions on the basis of feelings. People who are more thoughtful and less emotional may have difficulty maintaining intimacy, because intimacy requires sharing feelings and personal meaning about events. Persons with strong Thinking preference can enrich their marriage by practicing Discussions 1–6 in this chapter.

In contrast, people with a Feeling preference base their decisions and actions on how they feel about the matter, or how the decision will affect them and others on an emotional basis. Their loves and hates tend to be more visible and they recognize a strong need for intimacy. Those who have a strong Feeling preference may have difficulty thinking through issues on a rational basis and may not immediately understand the values and beliefs behind their emotional responses. They will inspire empathy from other people when they express emotions at a moderate level of intensity. However, if a Feeling person's emotions seem to be out of control, other people's empathy can turn to discomfort. Spouses with Feeling preference can enrich their marriages by engaging in activities that solve problems in their relationship, for instance, making clear requests and promises.

You can use your emotions as a gift to fully experience life and to make decisions that direct you toward greater fulfillment. Communicating emotions skillfully can draw you closer to your partner as you increase your ability to understand and express the emotional depth of your experience.

For Practice

1. Share feelings daily using, "You did _____, and I felt _____." Both spouses should share.

2. Set aside time daily to tell your spouse the important events in your day and the emotions evoked by those events. If you are the type that does not notice feelings, push yourself to notice subtle ones, such as satisfaction, contentment, comfort, confusion, or concern.

3. Celebrate the completion of Recreating Marriage.

NOTES

1. Michael E. Kerr and Murray Bowen, *Family Evaluation* (New York: W. W. Norton & Co., 1988).

2. Marjorie J. Thompson, *Soul Feast* (Louisville, Ky.: Westminster John Knox Press, 1995).

Conclusion

Congratulations on finishing Recreating Marriage. But your work on your marriage is not over. You need to continue asking the discussion questions of each other through the years. The answers change. What does love mean to you? For what do you want to be affirmed? In what ways do you wish I would support you? Why did you break that promise?

A continuously recreated relationship is one of God's most precious gifts. A loving marriage nurtures you to be the person God intended, to answer God's call. Commitment to marriage does not mean simply staying together. It means commitment to the identity, that sacred self, of both of you. You can use your talents by continuously giving yourself in a way that brings you joy in return. Within such a marriage, you do not need to use energy to protect yourself but, instead, can use your efforts for creative work.

Living most of your life with a person who is different from you is a big challenge. At first, when you are in love, you pretend that there are no differences. Then, after you have lived together for a while, you may feel all is lost because there are so *many* differences. Through this book, you have learned that there is hope that you can manage your differences and continue loving. You can balance each other because you are different from each other. Your differences add to the capabilities of the relationship rather than discouraging each other. Your differences challenge you to appreciate something that may not be natural to you, stretching your experience of life. Discussing differences challenges you to open your mind to consider another point of view.

As you give of yourself through listening, appreciating and affirming, making requests and making and keeping promises, and sharing your feelings, you develop a greater ability to give. As you give, you will receive, in return. The act of listening touches you as you receive your partner. Appreciating and affirming your partner calls your attention to the pleasure you receive. Requests open you to the possibility that you might receive what you want from your partner. In giving promises and keeping them, you, too, become more trustworthy. As you express your emotions, the love you feel opens your heart to a lifetime of health and joy.

For Further Reading

Richard D. Carson. *Taming Your Gremlin*. New York: HarperPerennial, 1983.

Gary Chapman. *The Five Love Languages*. Chicago: Northfield Publishing, 1992.

Mihaly Csikszentmihalyi. *Flow: The Psychology of Optimal Experience*. New York: Harper & Row, 1990.

Roger Fisher and Scott Brown. *Getting Together: Building Relationships as We Negotiate*. New York: Penguin Books, 1988.

Thomas Gordon. *Parent Effectiveness Training*. New York: Peter H. Wyden, 1970.

James Hillman. *The Soul's Code*. New York: Random House, 1996.

David Keirsey and Marilyn Bates. *Please Understand Me*. Del Mar, Calif.: Prometheus Nemesis Book Co., 1984.

Otto Kroeger and Janet M. Thresen. *Type Talk*. New York: Delacrote Press, 1988.

Jennifer Louden. *The Couple's Comfort Book*. San Francisco: HarperSanFrancisco, 1994.

Thomas Merton. *New Seeds of Contemplation*. New York: New Directions Publishing, 1972.

Marjorie J. Thompson. *Soul Feast*. Louisville, Ky.: Westminster John Knox Press, 1995.